THE ESSENCE OF LEADERSHIP

– UNVEILINGQUALITIES THAT INSPIRE

KAVIYARASU AYYAKANNU

ARS JAYANTH

Made with ❤ on the Notion Press Platform

www.notionpress.com

Motivational writers Nagalakshmi Shanmugam and Brian Tracy

Contents

Foreword

An English proverb states, 'A teacher is better than two books,' emphasizing the superior value of a teacher's guidance over mere book knowledge. Professor Kaviyarasu, the author of this book, exemplifies this sentiment through his recounting of academic experiences, interactions with notable personalities, and the insights gained from his ventures. Rather than simply presenting abstract ideas, he shares engaging narratives that resonate deeply with readers. My heartfelt congratulations to him for this achievement. The anecdotes shared in this book, such as the tale of the mountain slope or the parting of the sky, serve as catalysts for personal growth, inspiring readers to strive for more despite challenges or limitations. Professor Kaviyarasu's narrative style effectively communicates subtle lessons drawn from real-life events, affirming the adage that experience is indeed the best teacher. His writings not only impart knowledge but also instil confidence and motivation in readers, encouraging self-improvement. As his writing journey continues, I earnestly hope for his more insightful and inspiring works.

- Vijayakumar Tamilanban

15.05.2024

Preface

Across various languages globally, 'Leadership' stands as a remarkably beautiful term—a beacon of hope. This powerful word serves as an unparalleled force, bringing diverse minds together and guiding them towards shared goals. Bestowing the gift of experience is a key element for ensuring your success. Is this book on leadership qualities finding its way into your hands? If so, it indicates that you are on the verge of excelling in leadership. Within these pages, I've divulged strategies, actions, and essential leadership practices to enhance your capabilities. All of these insights have been distilled from my personal experiences, interactions with friends, readings, and engagement with social media.

I've penned this book with the aspiration that my modest experiences can aid individuals, such as yourself, aspiring to thrive in leadership, whether in certain situations, at particular junctures, or beyond. The influence of calligraphy in the realm of arts is profound, and throughout history, from the Stone Age to the present, humanity has harnessed writing as a potent instrument for conveying thoughts and documenting events. Commencing with primitive scribbles, humans have employed writing to convey their thoughts and ideas, adapting to technological advancements across different eras—from cave paintings and inscriptions to copper plates and printed copies. Recognizing, to a certain extent, the influential role of writing throughout human history, I was motivated to compile it into a book.

Upon deciding to venture into writing books, I found myself perplexed. What should be the subject of my books? A historical novel has always been a cherished aspiration of mine, yet up until now, I haven't been able to materialize this desire into concrete action. In addition to my decision to write a book on the fundamentals of Ham Radio and its applications, there was a sudden emergence of the idea for a book on the "Qualities of Leadership." This book encompasses a compilation of diverse individuals I've encountered, their experiences, insights into the functioning of Anna University, my own experiences within the Internal Quality Assurance Cell (IQAC), various approaches, strategies employed, and more.

I'm aware that there might be some scepticism about my knowledge of leadership qualities, especially considering my background primarily focused on classroom and home research rather than management and leadership. I understand how someone with a limited interest in these areas can write a book on leadership and its characteristics. In 2022, I stepped into leadership for the first time, initially assuming the role of the campus coordinator at the Internal Quality Assurance (IQAC). Later that same year, I took on the position of deputy director. This marks my initial experience in leadership, to emphasize, encompassing less than a year's worth of insights.

I did not have direct leadership experience until 2022, in a way. But one of my strengths is the ability to delve deeper into any subject, absorb it experientially, and put it into practice. I have written this book to make others aware of the experiences I have gained by combining the basic knowledge acquired in this way with the ability to act and apply it to the leadership qualities offered.

"Every experience you get and the understanding that comes with it are factors that can make your foundation stronger"

My initiation into leadership unfolded within the precincts of Anna University's Internal Quality Assurance Cell (IQAC). The pivotal roles of Anna University and IQAC have shaped my understanding of leadership qualities. I extend my sincere gratitude to the Hon'ble Dr. Velraj Ramalingam, the Vice-Chancellor of the University, for providing me with this opportunity. Additionally, my thanks go to the Registrar, Dr. Prakash Jagadeesan, and the Head of the Department, Dr.

Paramasivam. Special acknowledgment is due to Dr. Gunasekaran Raja, Director of IQAC, and my esteemed colleagues, including Major Suresh Babu, Dr. Perarasu, Dr. Sangeetha, Dr. Bhagavathyammal, Dr. Indira Gandhi, Dr. Shanthakumar, and all the dedicated staff at IQAC.

To me, leadership isn't solely defined by enduring authority and power. Conversely, reaching the pinnacle of leadership occurs when you find fulfillment in others' success and their elevation to greater heights. The fundamental essence of leadership lies in leading a purposeful life for the benefit of others. Those who embrace the teachings of Buddha and walk the path of righteousness epitomize the qualities of Buddha's leadership. Regardless of religious affiliations, everyone embodying the virtues of their faith and adhering to ethical principles possesses a form of leadership within. The key is to awaken this dormant leadership within you. Recognize that you are inherently endowed with boundless leadership potential. Cultivate the latent energies within and endeavor to unleash them into the vast expanse of freedom. After all, you are born to achieve, designed by a higher power to manifest creative endeavors.

One memorable day, I strolled alongside my esteemed grandfather, Mr. Govindan, a retired school headmaster, when a white Ambassador vehicle halted at a distance. Adorned in a white dhoti, a gentleman alighted from the vehicle and walked directly towards us. He humbly touched my grandfather's feet, seeking his blessings. Upon inquiring about the visitor, we learned that he currently serves as a judge in the Madras High Court and is an alumnus of my grandfather. Expressing warmth, he invited my grandfather to his nearby residence. Despite the challenges of old age affecting his memory, my grandfather greeted him wholeheartedly and bid him farewell.

The pinnacle of human achievement lies solely in the realm of education. No other pursuit in the world can ascend to such heights of excellence. Education is the supreme beacon, dispelling the darkness of ignorance and casting the radiant light of knowledge upon our lives. According to my grandfather, education is the one subject that people willingly share and appreciate with others. He emphasized that engaging in the noble teaching profession is a source of pride, a divine opportunity bestowed upon us by the higher powers. It was my grandfather who redirected my aspirations from joining the Military Defence and Research Department towards embracing the teaching profession, and for that, I owe him my gratitude.

Kaviyarasu Ayyakannu

15.05.2024

Acknowledgments

I extend my deepest gratitude to Mr. Vijayakumar Thamizhanban, my writer and student friend, whose encouragement was the catalyst for embarking on the journey of writing this book. My heartfelt thanks are dedicated to my pillar of strength, my wife Ragavi, and to my unwavering support system - My father Ayyakannu, mother Karpagam, brothers Karthik and Kabilan, and the ever-enthusiastic Master Siranjivi. Their inspiration and steadfast support have not only fueled my various activities but also played an integral role in helping me rediscover and connect with my true self.

1. Anna University and Internal Quality Assurance Cell

To fully grasp my evolution into leadership, it's crucial to delve into the backdrop of Anna University and the formative influence of the IQAC on my leadership qualities. Consequently, the initial chapters of this book are dedicated to unraveling the intricacies of Anna University, the establishment of the IQAC, and its operational dynamics. I find it necessary to present these details not only to enhance public awareness of Anna University but also to ensure that you, the reader, can embark on this journey alongside me with a comprehensive understanding.

Anna University is a merger comprising four campuses, viz. the College of Engineering Guindy (CEG) Campus, the Madras Institute of Technology (MIT) Campus, the Alagappa College of Technology (ACT) Campus, and the School of Architecture and Planning (SAP) Campus. Among them, only the Madras Institute of Technology (MIT) is situated in Chromepet, near Tambaram, covering approximately 52 acres along GST Road. It was established in July 1949 by the late industrialist Mr. Rajam. The college was later merged with Anna University. The additional campuses, namely, College of Engineering Guindy, Alagappa College of Technology, and School of

Architecture and Planning, are situated on approximately 189 acres near Sardar Patel Road in Guindy. Alagappa College of Technology was started by Mr. Alagappa Chettiar in 1944, before India's independence. The SAP campus was started in 1957. It is the first technical college to be established for Architecture in India. Guindy Engineering College was established in 1794 to serve the requirements of the British Government during the 18th century. It started as the "School of Survey" and later incorporated various technical and engineering disciplines, such as Civil Engineering and Mechanical Engineering. Distinguished as Asia's oldest Technical College and the first Technical University outside of Europe, it has consistently demonstrated excellence in academic pursuits globally.

In tribute to the late Former Chief Minister of Tamil Nadu, Hon'ble C.N. Annadurai, these campuses were consolidated and rebranded as Perarignar Anna Technological University (now Anna University) on October 4, 1978, inaugurated by the then President, Neelam Sanjeeva Reddy. The establishment of the university was orchestrated under the leadership of former Chief Minister M.G. Ramachandran. Prof. P. Sivalingam, hailing from Melur village in Madurai district, assumed the role of its inaugural Vice-Chancellor.

Following P. Sivalingam, approximately eleven distinguished professors have held the position of Vice-Chancellor at Anna University. Each of them exhibited exceptional qualities and distinctive leadership, contributing significantly to the development and foundational structure of the university. Under their guidance, Anna University has attained numerous accomplishments, aligning with global standards. Notably, the university played a pivotal role in introducing the

"Single Window Counselling System" to the world. It is now widely adopted by the All-India Institute of Medical Sciences (AIIMS) and many universities in the neighbouring states for their counselling processes.

Anna University has achieved a significant milestone with the launch of ANUSAT, which stands for Anna University Satellite, the world's first student satellite mission, in 2009. Developed entirely by Anna University students with the support of the Indian Space Research Organisation (ISRO), ANUSAT was successfully launched using a PSLV-C12 launch vehicle. Recognizing the global impact of its academic disciplines, the University Grants Commission (UGC), in its XI direction, acknowledged the Department of Biomedical Engineering and Instrumentation at Anna University as an emerging field worldwide. This recognition came with substantial financial support to elevate the department to international standards, setting Anna University apart among the fifteen selected universities in India.

In another pioneering feat, Anna University holds the distinguished status of being the first university granted permission by the Directorate General of Civil Aviation (DGCA) to conduct training programs for Drones in the field of Drone technology. Beyond these achievements, Anna University houses various unique research centers, including globally acclaimed institutions such as the Institute of Remote Sensing (IRS), The Crystal Growth Centre, the Centre for Education and Multimedia Research (EMMRC), the National Hub for Healthcare Instrumentation Development (NHHID), and the Institute for Energy Studies (IES). These centers exemplify the university's commitment to cutting-edge research and innovation.

Anna University holds the distinction of not only establishing the groundwork for the Indian Engineering sector by pioneering undergraduate courses in Mechanical, Electrical Engineering, and Aerospace Engineering during the inception of the Engineering field in India but also consistently producing some of the globe's top engineers and technologists. As per the Quacquerelli Symonds (QS) World Rankings, Anna University has made progress in its position from 289th Rank in 2023 to 249th Rank in 2024, under the category Engineering and Technology, among the best universities in the world. This remarkable journey has been made possible through meticulous planning, outstanding leadership guidance, and the unwavering commitment of the university's dedicated staff.

The National Assessment and Accreditation Council (NAAC) play a pivotal role in evaluating and ranking the performance of Higher Educational Institutions (HEI) in India. As an autonomous body funded by the University Grants Commission (UGC) and the Government of India (GOI), with its headquarters in Bangalore, NAAC was established in 1994 following the recommendations of the National Education Policy (NEP) enacted in 1986. The overarching goal of this education policy is to identify and rectify deficiencies in the quality of education within higher learning institutions.

To this end, NAAC formulates various action plans designed to elevate the standards of higher educational institutions and address their shortcomings. Instituting quality certifications, particularly through in-person inspections of the best-performing institutions, is a key aspect of this process. These certifications are crucial for institutions to secure funds from the Central Government.

In line with the NAAC directive issued in 2018, every educational institution, including Anna University, was required to establish an Internal Quality Assurance Cell (IQAC) and outline its functioning. Consequently, Anna University's IQAC, formerly associated with Planning and Development (P&D), transitioned into an independent center in 2018.

The organization's primary functions extend beyond internal improvement, aiming to secure National Assessment Board Certification (NAAC Certification), National Accreditation Board (NBA) accreditation, and approval for vocational courses from the All-India Council for Technical Education (AICTE). Actively participating in global academic ranking competitions such as Quacquarelli Symonds (QS) and Times Higher Education (THE), as well as the National Institute Ranking Framework (NIRF), underscores the commitment to excellence.

A crucial responsibility of the Internal Quality Assurance Cell is the ongoing engagement in planning activities geared towards enhancing the quality of higher education, as evidenced by the obtained rankings and accreditations.

****

2. Why NAAC and NBA?

Everywhere I go, one question is consistently directed at me, a question that often crosses the minds of many staff members at the university: "Now that we've become a state educational institution, do we really need these recognitions and evaluations?" Before delving into an answer, allow me to share a brief anecdote.

In a town, there lived a father and son. As the son reached adulthood, he expressed his desire to become self-employed. Despite the father's extreme poverty, he handed over the watch gifted to him by his father to support his son's venture. Instructing him to sell the watch, the son approached a nearby shop, only to be offered a mere 20 rupees by the shopkeeper, who dismissed it as an old, broken timepiece. Disheartened, the son sought his father's advice. The father, unimpressed by the meagre sum, suggested consulting a watch shop instead. This time, the shop employee recognized the true worth of the watch and offered 400 rupees. Still dissatisfied, the son consulted his father once more, who proposed visiting the Archaeological Museum on the next street.

To their astonishment, the museum employee appraised the watch at a staggering 75 lakh rupees, revealing its historical significance and unique features. Overwhelmed, the son recounted the events to his father. The father, who had been quietly observing, imparted a valuable lesson. "My dear son, I didn't give you the watch to sell it. Instead, I gave it to you to illustrate the importance of placing an object where it belongs. The true value of an object becomes apparent when it is in its rightful place. Therefore, choose places and actions that add value to your life. This is what will propel you forward."

In the same vein, the university's pursuit of recognitions and evaluations may seem challenging at times, but their true worth becomes evident when placed in the context of enhancing the institution's overall value and contributing to its advancement.

Rankings and accreditations serve as valuable tools for assessing the competencies of Higher Educational Institutions. By incorporating best practices from other institutions into their own education systems, universities can enhance the quality of education they offer to their communities. In today's modern era, where continuous improvement and self-assessment are imperative, recognition and ranking systems play a crucial role in evaluating universities' effectiveness and fostering learning outcomes.

Just as the father advised his son, these recognitions and rankings allow institutions to showcase their quality and value to the wider world. Furthermore, they are vital for securing funding from entities such as the Department of Higher Education, the Government of India, and the All-India Council for Technical Education, underscoring their significance in the broader landscape of higher education.

All rankings and accreditations are contingent upon the data provided to the respective agencies. The actions undertaken by the university significantly influence its ranking and recognition. To excel in this realm, active engagement in collective endeavours, commonly referred to as "Teamwork," is indispensable. Timely receipt of information from various departments and research centers is imperative for active participation in rankings and accreditations, ultimately contributing to the organization's enhanced efficiency. Any delays or insufficient information in this regard can have adverse consequences.

I would like to draw attention to the challenges posed by the 2023-NAAC and 2023-NIRF assessments, which are deemed to be among the most demanding tasks encountered. Handling the information pertinent to NAAC and NIRF received from the offices of the principals (Deans) can be overwhelming, at times even perplexing. To share a discreet insight, it is not uncommon for individuals working in the IQAC to experience hair loss, particularly at the front, owing to the intricate nature of these tasks.

When seeking information on the number of first-year students in higher education institutions, disparities arise between data sourced from the Dean's office, the admission center, and a specialized center like the NRI information center. Each dataset contradicts the others, occasionally leading to unexpected surprises.

Typically, information from the offices under your purview tends to arrive belatedly. Despite numerous reminders, phone conversations, and correspondences, the updates trickle in at a pace reminiscent of a Tiruvarur chariot. Consequently, the last-minute influx renders the information practically futile for both you and your organization. Instead of enabling thoughtful and informed decision-making, it compels a mindset that deems the mere arrival of information as sufficient. Navigating such situations requires a combination of patience, restraint, and careful attention.

This challenge becomes particularly pronounced when dealing with the submission of information for NIRF and QS. While the information may seem accurate upon receipt, discrepancies and distortions, when compared to data from the previous year, appear glaringly problematic. Being prepared to take immediate action during such instances is essential. It necessitates proactive preparation of various information in advance.

Occasionally, your employees may express dissatisfaction, citing contradictions among the information you request. Such occurrences are not uncommon, and frustration may even arise within yourself. However, it is crucial to recognize that this process serves the purpose of allowing them to verify and rectify last-minute information. Providing comprehensive explanations to your employees in advance regarding the information you require whenever feasible is an invaluable strategy. This approach represents an unparalleled effort that can elicit the best performance from your team, propelling both you and your team toward success.

****

3. Recognition of Labour

The human mind does not instinctively focus on recognizing the actions and consequences resulting from diligent efforts. Instead, it tends to initially emphasize the faults and inherent flaws in one's actions. Such a unique circumstance became apparent during the initial stages of the NAAC-2023 data validation process. At that point, the majority of the NAAC data collection work had been concluded. To ensure the accuracy of the compiled information, we organized an internal review, inviting a group of university professors to scrutinize our findings.

This team of professors meticulously analyzed all the gathered information, posing a series of questions to which we provided comprehensive answers based on our knowledge. Prior to the review, we had briefed the team on the evaluation and scoring criteria, and they unanimously accepted our explanations. Upon the conclusion of the internal review, the team expressed appreciation for our efforts, extended their gratitude, and departed. However, some people think that the IQAC team seemed to be addressing NAAC-related matters without a complete understanding.

No matter how hard you work for your company's growth beyond your capacity, a few people around you can easily blame your actions and hard work. I strongly recommend, leave such negative critics and focus more on your actions. People like them are "Negative" and do not seek to do anything. They will continue to sow negative thoughts by finding faults. It is advisable to steer clear of encountering such individuals in any situation.

Our team, along with myself, dedicated extensive hours to the NAAC accreditation process. We tirelessly fostered awareness and comprehension of NAAC among all university stakeholders, making it a prolonged and challenging endeavour. Reflecting on this journey, it is truly remarkable how we achieved this feat. In the midst of such diligent work, we were heartened to witness the voluntary participation of 35 departments, 90 research centers, and over 2,000 human resources. It is a testament to the collective effort and the willingness of the entire organization and its employees to actively contribute when engaged in activities that ultimately benefit the organization.

When reflecting on our accomplishments through IQAC, we choose not to emphasize our ascent in QS ranking, the elevation in NIRF ranking, or the attainment of seven years of NAAC and six years of NBA accreditation. Instead, we celebrate our team's most notable triumph: fostering a comprehensive understanding of these achievements among all stakeholders of Anna University. This feat is not to be underestimated. It entails instilling such comprehension across a university where over 2,000 staff members converge—a task that demands meticulous planning and unwavering dedication. Direct communication with our employees is paramount in this endeavour.

In essence, how can we accomplish these feats?

Initially, we uplifted our staff, who were teetering on the brink of despair, by highlighting the University's progress and achievements stemming from their noble efforts. Then, we engaged directly with them, lending explanation and listening attentively to their feedback. We countered their negative sentiments with our positive outlook, meticulously choosing our words to infuse encouragement. Recognizing the importance of refining our oratory skills, we took deliberate steps in that direction. Making it a daily practice to familiarize ourselves with pertinent data about individuals we interacted with proved invaluable, enabling us to gather insights and connect more effectively.

Recognizing the importance of fostering a direct connection with Anna University staff, we embarked on a proactive plan. Leveraging the Indian Research Information Network System (IRINS), an online information management service developed by the Indian Information and Library Network Centre, became our initial strategy. Since its inception in 2007, IRINS has served to integrate research, funding, papers, and intellectual property innovations from educational institutions across India. Despite Anna University's membership, awareness among stakeholders remained lacking. Prof. Gunasekaran Raja, IQAC Director, and Prof. Arivudainambi, Library Director, spearheaded the initiative to enhance understanding and utilization of IRINS. We engaged directly with all employees, elucidating its services and benefits for both individuals and departments. The reception was overwhelmingly positive, with unexpected outcomes emerging as employees began actively participating, contributing data, and highlighting challenges. Dr.

Krishnamurthy and Dr. Kothainayaki, assistant librarians, played a pivotal role in refining this process.

We substantially expanded our faculty, increasing from 407 to 907 members, as we diligently pursued our objectives. Our research output saw a remarkable surge, with the number of organized research papers escalating from 12,334 to 21,880. Additionally, we elevated the recommendations of research articles in Scopus from 1,53,661 to 2,17,848, and in Cross-reference from 89,090 to 1,97,279. Demonstrating our commitment to intellectual property rights, we bolstered indices from 22 to 277. These achievements resonated in the QS and NIRF rankings for the year. Notably, according to the 2023 NIRF rankings, we leaped into the top 15 in the Research, Engineering, and Universities categories, a substantial improvement from the previous year. Furthermore, our Global QS ranking soared from 801-1000 to 427, securing a place among India's top 10 universities.

Sony's mantra

Akio Morita, the visionary founder of Sony, revolutionized the electronics industry by imprinting the company's name, "Sony," and the phrase "Made in Japan" in golden letters. Following World War II, he shattered the misconception that Japan could only produce inferior goods like cheap sports equipment and umbrellas, introducing high-quality electronics to the world. Morita's pioneering role in inventing and popularizing products such as tape recorders, Walkman, and video cassette players was extraordinary.

In his autobiography, Morita reflects on his journey, emphasizing the crucial role of effective communication in sales. He underscores the necessity of reaching the right audience with the right products, drawing from his first-hand experience selling tape recorders. Morita highlights a flaw in the traditional Japanese trade system, where goods were solely sold through intermediaries, resulting in a disconnect between manufacturers and end-users. Recognizing the importance of educating consumers about the utility of their products, Morita and Sony took the lead in directly engaging with customers, thus becoming trailblazers in product sales and innovation.

Akio Morita and Anna University

Akio Morita's strategic approach served as our guiding principle during the data collection process for NIRF, NBA, IRINS, and NAAC accreditation. Our first step was to cultivate a sense of harmony between the informants and the stakeholders. We personally visited every department, laboratory, and faculty member, elucidating the significance of pursuing recognition and rankings. We emphasized the tangible benefits that such efforts would yield for them. Throughout this endeavour, my team and I remained undeterred by potential challenges, focusing wholeheartedly on our actions. In instances where information was elusive, we left no stone unturned, engaging in discussions, meetings, and necessary steps to bridge any gaps.

While we may not have an immediate answer to whether our initiative directly led to NAAC A++ accreditation, one thing became abundantly clear to all stakeholders of our university: their involvement and contribution are integral to our collective success. The positive feedback and appreciation received from the university bolstered our resolve and revitalized our efforts. To this day, we regard this initiative as the pinnacle of our endeavours at IQAC.

****

4. Effort towards the Goal

Progressing toward your goals stands as a pivotal phase in your journey towards leadership. It serves to both shape and refine your leadership qualities, while also affording opportunities to adapt management strategies to align with the mindset of your employees. Establishing a harmonious environment between management and staff emerges as a strategic approach to expedite goal attainment. Embracing the norm as a proactive measure can pave the way for ordinary employees to transcend into extraordinary achievers. Should you excel in leadership qualities and command the allegiance of your team, adjusting certain habits becomes imperative to ensure your objectives are realized. Let's further discuss the steps necessary to navigate towards achieving your goals.

Get started with ease

Film Director Mr.S.J.Surya once imparted, "We must persevere in our endeavours, regardless of the obstacles we encounter. Even when faced with darkness, take a step forward, and the path will illuminate itself. The journey itself, not just the destination, holds its own joys." These words resonate deeply with me, reflecting the invaluable lessons gleaned from my time at IQAC. When undertaking challenging tasks, begin by embracing them with contentment, then proceed to methodically plan their execution. If initial efforts yield modest results, remain undeterred. Instead, accept them as they are and discard the notion that success is contingent upon achieving perfection from the outset. Persist in your efforts, and you'll find that your actions evolve far beyond your initial expectations. This ethos mirrors our approach to the NAAC accreditation process, embodying our commitment to continual improvement and resilience in the face of challenges.

This year, our approach to NAAC accreditation has been more systematic than ever before. Initially, we segmented the various components involved in the NAAC evaluation process and devised comprehensive plans for each. The NAAC framework comprises 7 metric divisions and 115 subdivisions, including both Qualitative and Quantitative Metrics (QNM and QLM). QNM entails compiling five years worth of data, while QLM involves providing detailed written commentary on this data.

Collating information from 35 Departments and 90 Research Centers posed a significant challenge. Potential pitfalls included discrepancies in gathered information, insufficient supporting sources, and delays from certain departments and research centers. To navigate these obstacles effectively, meticulous planning and patience were paramount. Ensuring the accuracy and validity of the information collected was crucial to securing favourable marks for the university.

Avoid assigning blame

The intricacies of the human brain are unparalleled, capable of transcending the challenges posed by modern science and technology. Human thoughts possess a remarkable adaptability to circumstances, drawing upon memories and shadow time to make spontaneous decisions that shape future development. These processes are often influenced by external factors such as parental legacy, environmental cycles, and situational dynamics, rather than inherent individual characteristics. Therefore, refrain from attributing blame to others. Instead, focus on embracing their strengths while letting go of any shortcomings. Consider how these strengths can be harnessed to foster company growth, thereby enhancing the positive energy of your leadership qualities.

Refrain from disseminating unfounded misinformation

As a leader, it's imperative to refrain from sharing unsubstantiated and false information, as doing so can severely damage your reputation and credibility. Recently, in my college WhatsApp group, a friend shared a message regarding India's 74th Independence Day celebrations. The message claimed that the British granted independence on August 15, 2018, as it coincided with a full moon day, in response to Indian demands. However, a quick check of the Tamil version of the monthly online calendar revealed that there was no full moon on that day, debunking the claim. It became evident that my friend had blindly accepted misinformation without verifying its accuracy, inadvertently perpetuating falsehoods. Such instances highlight the dangers of spreading unchecked information, which can further entrench falsehoods in society. Instead, it's crucial to approach information critically, relying on knowledge to discern truth from falsehood rather than accepting information at face value.

On November 6, 2016, the government made a significant announcement: Rs 500 and Rs 1,000 currency notes would cease to be legal tender as part of the demonetization initiative. In their place, the Reserve Bank of India (RBI) introduced new Rs 2,000 banknotes, boasting sophisticated design and enhanced security features. However, amidst this transition, unfounded rumours began circulating, suggesting that these new notes contained electronic chips detectable by satellites. These baseless claims gained traction, amplified by several celebrities on social media platforms.

One ordinary individual, the owner of my residence, approached me seeking clarification on this matter. Despite my explanation that current technology couldn't accommodate micro-sized chips in banknotes or enable their detection via GPS, he remained convinced. Pointing to the image of the Mangalyaan mission on the back of the Rs 2,000 note, he insisted that the government had implemented such measures. Instead of reacting with frustration, I felt a sense of compassion toward those misled by misinformation.

This incident underscored the harmful impact of unchecked rumours and misinformation, exacerbating issues rather than seeking solutions. It serves as a reminder of the importance of critically evaluating information before accepting it as truth.

As a leader, you may occasionally encounter falsehoods and hoaxes. In such situations, it's essential to respond with composure and a commitment to dispelling ignorance. Your aim should be to educate rather than to chastise, ensuring that individuals' sentiments are respected throughout the process.

These misconceptions often proliferate through various channels such as social gatherings, motivational seminars, and public speeches. They stem from the inadvertent repetition of ideas without critical analysis or consideration of one's knowledge. While it's challenging to eradicate such falsehoods entirely, they persist in various forms and situations. As a responsible leader, prioritize avoiding the propagation of misconceptions and misinformation. Instead, strive to foster an environment of critical thinking and informed decision-making among your team members.

At times, individuals seize opportunities presented by events to benefit themselves, others, and their organization, showcasing exceptional management skills. Administration, however, is not an individual endeavour but a collective effort, akin to an expansive ocean where diverse ideas and perspectives converge. If one merely stands on the shore, they can admire the ocean's beauty, but by diving in, they can explore its depths and uncover its myriad treasures. Whether one chooses to remain on the shore or dive into the depths is a personal decision that shapes their experience. The ocean serves as a reflective mirror, portraying one's mindset and perspective.

Approaching activities with understanding and a thirst for knowledge adds value and elevates them to a higher level. Without genuine interest, endeavours are unlikely to achieve their objectives.

****

5. Harmonise the Collective Energy

The greatest power we have is our potential. By nurturing and guiding it in the right direction, we can achieve great things. The key is to identify the unique talents of each person and assign tasks that align with those strengths. We should also strive to inspire and teach those around us, helping them to see the value of their contributions and how their work can improve their own lives and the lives of others. By creating a supportive and communicative environment, we can help people reach their full potential.

Are you going to be involved in challenging project tasks? First, fully understand the ideas and actions involved in the project. Plan how to complete the activity efficiently and effectively. Then, explain the project activities to your team and how they should be carried out. Explore how these actions will improve your team's abilities. Explain the value and impact of their contributions to the project. By following these steps, you can quickly improve the performance of different groups or individuals. These actions are considered essential for building understanding between you and your team members.

Understanding can foster attraction between people. It allows for improved collaboration and better results in various endeavours. By developing a deeper understanding, you can achieve your goals more swiftly and efficiently.

Our discussion has focused on understanding in the workplace. Now, let's shift our focus to the human mind and the challenges it presents. In leadership, understanding the human mind is considered essential.

Is a comprehensive understanding of the human mind essential?

Effective leadership hinges on understanding the complexities of the human mind. The human mind is remarkably adaptable, able to adjust its thinking and motivations in response to different circumstances. This adaptability can be a source of strength, as exemplified by my friend who initially aspired to be a newsreader but ultimately found fulfilment in teaching. However, it can also lead to inconsistency, and you may encounter colleagues or employees whose thoughts and goals seem to fluctuate. In such situations, empathy is key. By seeking to understand their perspectives and thought processes, you can foster a productive working relationship. Actively listen to their ideas and provide constructive feedback to help them develop their skills. Highlight the potential benefits of their current approach and acknowledge the challenges they may face in a new direction. Similarly, emphasize their strengths in their previous role and the unique value they bring to the team. Effectively understanding your employees is an art, but one that can be mastered through consistent effort and focused communication.

Minor changes can lead to significant improvements

To effectively reach your goals, it's imperative to wholeheartedly recognize and acknowledge the small efforts and actions of your team members. Take, for instance, my experience as the Deputy Director of IQAC, where we prioritized direct engagement with each department during the NAAC data collection process. Our approach involved not only explaining the intricacies of the software and data requirements but also fostering a sense of psychological connection.

This undertaking wasn't just a task; it was a strategic manoeuvre that demanded extra effort. We personally visited every Department and Research Center, totalling 35 departments and 90 research and administrative centers. This hands-on approach served multiple purposes. Firstly, it allowed us to establish rapport and familiarity with each team. Additionally, it conveyed a clear message: we valued their role as much as our own, particularly in the upcoming NAAC 2023 endeavour.

This approach yielded substantial benefits. By directly engaging with every entity, we not only introduced ourselves and our methodologies but also emphasized the significance of their contributions. This collaborative mindset fostered a sense of ownership and commitment among the teams, ultimately enhancing our collective efforts towards achieving our objectives.

During the NAAC 2023 data collection endeavour, the meticulous efforts of Professors Srirangarajalu and Mugendiran, hailing from the Department of Production Technology, and Kavitha Ganesan, a luminary in the Department of Electronics, left an indelible mark on our team. Their subtle yet significant contributions laid the groundwork for future information-gathering endeavours within the university.

I had the privilege of being mentored by Professor Kavitha Ganesan during my post-graduate studies. His unwavering commitment to excellence is truly commendable; she approaches every task with a dedication to surpassing expectations. Professor Srirangarajalu's expertise in planning is unparalleled. His adeptness at formulating and executing plans with precision is a testament to his outstanding capabilities. As for Professor Mugendiran, he epitomizes the ethos of 'Karmaveer'—a fearless doer who plunges into action without hesitation or reservation.

Their remarkable performances reflect their innate leadership qualities and underscore their innate commitment to excellence. It's as if their predisposition for exceptional performance was ingrained in them from birth. In essence, their contributions exemplify excellence and inspire all who endeavor to achieve greatness.

The examples I have shared here are but a glimpse of the remarkable individuals I've had the privilege to collaborate with. Through my interactions with them, I've come to appreciate their unique personalities and unwavering dedication to the advancement of our university. However, it's important to acknowledge that there are many more individuals who, like them, tirelessly contribute to the growth and development of our institution.

I regret that, due to oversight, I haven't mentioned all of them here. I take full responsibility for this omission. Moving forward, I aspire to recognize and celebrate the efforts of all those who labour selflessly for the betterment of our university community.

As I reflect on these experiences, I'm humbled and hopeful. I fervently pray to the Divine that I may continue to encounter extraordinary individuals with diverse energies and talents, individuals whose collective efforts propel our university to greater heights.

Anna University's global reputation is a testament to the boundless dedication of such compassionate souls, who work tirelessly for the betterment of their respective fields and the overarching development of our alma mater, transcending personal interests for the greater good.

"We have a purpose to fulfil, and we will continue to strive for it"

A pivotal trait for aspiring leaders is their ability to impart knowledge and inspire learning among their subordinates. As the saying goes, "When you're at the hearth, you automatically pick up the ember" (an analogy highlighting the transfer of knowledge and skills from superior to subordinate). As a leader, it's imperative to be proficient in various domains; only then will your team be motivated to glean insights from you. Your journey towards leadership commences with honing your own skill set. Therefore, devote special attention to identifying and refining your abilities, as they will serve as invaluable assets on your leadership path. Moreover, the knowledge and skills imparted to your employees extend beyond the realm of mere job assignments, enriching their professional growth.

Hone your abilities (Refine your abilities)

In the realm of administrative management, Mentor-Mentee tradition, assumes paramount significance. This system thrives on a profound symbiosis between the learner and the mentor. When this synergy is cultivated effectively, every action undertaken becomes inherently value-added.

Much like a diamond extracted from the earth initially appears lackluster, its true worth is realized only after undergoing meticulous polishing in the workshop. The crucial point to emphasize here is the inherent brilliance of the diamond. The more adeptly it is cut and polished in the workshop, the greater its value is appreciated.

Two crucial actions are imperative for maximizing the total value of the mined diamond: the cutting process and the expertise of the cutter. It is through the collective efforts of the craftsman and the cutter that the diamond attains its pinnacle of value. Similarly, in organizational dynamics, the concerted efforts of both the workforce and the leadership amplify the value of their actions.

Are you ready to refine yourself? Take action promptly. The first step is selecting your leader wisely—a pivotal decision that sets the stage for your journey toward leadership. Exercise utmost discernment in this choice, as it profoundly impacts your trajectory. While some decisions may not yield the desired outcomes, each situation offers invaluable lessons and experiences. Mastering the art of navigating these challenges creatively will pave the way for your ascension as a formidable leader in due course.

Employees and their collaboration form the bedrock of effective administrative operations. They constitute the backbone of the organization, and it takes astute leadership to elevate their routine tasks into value-added contributions. When both elements synergize seamlessly, the company's growth is palpably reflected in enhanced performance.

Professor Gunasekaran epitomizes exemplary leadership within our team. His profound contemplation is evident in every decision he makes, fostering an environment where diverse perspectives are not only welcomed but encouraged. He possesses a rare knack for discerning the unique strengths of each team member and proactively offers tailored suggestions to further enhance their capabilities.

Working under his guidance is akin to embarking on a journey of continual surprises. Professor Gunasekaran excels in simplifying complex tasks, offering accessible avenues for action. Yet, he also embodies resilience, never shying away from the rigors of hard work. Along this journey, you may find yourself feeling the weight of responsibility until the very end. However, it's in embracing this pressure that one discovers the latent leadership qualities within.

It's a testament to his mentorship that none of the employees who have worked alongside him have lost their innate leadership prowess. Under his tutelage, they blossom into formidable leaders in their own right, perpetuating a legacy of excellence and innovation.

One of the hallmark features of Anna University is its autonomous departmental structure. Under this system, each department operates with a high degree of independence and self-governance. This autonomy empowers departments to execute materials procurement or recruitment initiatives in accordance with university guidelines, thereby fostering a culture of spontaneity and productivity.

If you were to ask me the secret behind Anna University's remarkable growth, I would attribute it to this very system. The ability to function autonomously enables the university to undertake a plethora of constructive activities without unnecessary delays, ultimately enhancing overall productivity. This framework facilitates prompt decision-making, ensuring the well-being of both students and university staff.

However, it's important to acknowledge that effective communication poses a significant challenge within such an autonomous setup. Maintaining seamless communication channels between departments and the central administration remains an ongoing endeavour, essential for the smooth functioning of the university as a cohesive entity.

Navigating administrative hurdles when it comes to sharing information across different departments can be quite challenging. While accessing information within your own department might be relatively straightforward, obtaining details from other departments often entails a cumbersome process. Not only does this lead to time wastage, but it can also impede workflow efficiency, causing delays in essential tasks.

Waiting for weeks to acquire necessary information can significantly disrupt your plans and activities, hindering the timely completion of tasks. Any delay in action diminishes its effectiveness, ultimately affecting overall performance. It's crucial to recognize that seemingly insignificant time wastage can gradually erode productivity.

To foster a culture of efficiency and creativity, it's imperative to prioritize time management starting today. Set an example through your actions; for instance, if you typically arrive at college by 8:30 a.m., aim to arrive by 8:00 a.m. instead. This simple adjustment can save you valuable time, eliminating the need to rush to class and providing you with an extra half-hour for preparation.

Utilizing this additional time wisely, you can enhance your teaching methodologies by revisiting and refining lesson plans. By optimizing time management practices, you'll not only streamline administrative processes but also elevate the quality of your work, enabling you to deliver lessons more effectively.

Organizing your workload into categories of urgency—urgent, very urgent, and not urgent—can significantly streamline your tasks, ensuring that you prioritize effectively and meet deadlines efficiently. This structured approach not only simplifies your workflow but also serves as a constant reminder of impending deadlines.

In today's digital age, where mobile phones and laptops are ubiquitous, leverage the convenience of "Auto Inform" features available on your gadgets. These automated reminders can seamlessly integrate with your schedule, prompting you about upcoming tasks, meetings, and other commitments. By utilizing such tools, you can proactively manage your time and avoid instances of missed meetings or overlooked activities.

By implementing these strategies, you'll not only enhance your productivity but also cultivate a more organized and efficient work routine. Embracing modern technology empowers you to stay on top of your responsibilities, ensuring that you fulfil your professional obligations promptly and effectively.

****

6. Task Management

The core aim of integrating human capabilities is to inspire and enable your team to achieve greatness. The human mind possesses an unparalleled capacity to navigate emotions, seamlessly adapting to diverse scenarios like familial dynamics and professional environments. Thus, humanity is still achieving many extraordinary achievements in the face of various circumstances and various activities. Regarding work management, employees should focus on their time and engage in mind-blowing activities such as good ideas, conversations, fun, dancing, etc., from time to time. This is a strategy that brings people together psychologically. It is challenging to put yourself in front of your employees in the first place. However, you need to consider the benefits and take steps to implement it. While these may seem unnecessary when you approach them superficially, they give rise to various creative activities that can add value. They help us perform multiple positive production functions, starting with individual discipline, team unity, and administrative skills.

Ergonomic work-table configuration

In my experience as an IQAC Deputy Director, I was pleasantly surprised by the high-quality computer provided at my workstation. The 27-inch screen required some adjustment after previously using a 17-inch monitor on a smaller desk. When I inquired about this, IQAC Director Professor Gunasekaran discussed the importance of productivity and how it can be significantly enhanced by providing employees with essential resources to perform their duties effectively. He emphasized that employee performance can improve substantially by ensuring they have access to modern equipment. This resonated with me, and I believe it's important to encourage employees to take advantage of the resources provided to maximize their productivity. By investing in modern infrastructure and ensuring employees understand how to use it effectively, organizations can experience significant gains in productivity.

Upgrade our infrastructure

Upgrading your company's infrastructure requires careful planning. Effective planning is paramount in this process. It entails careful consideration of all stakeholders' perspectives, weighing their strengths, weaknesses, and potential outcomes. Thorough exploration is necessary before taking decisive action, which should be expedited for swift implementation. Of utmost importance is active involvement in financial resource management.

As an illustration, while I compose this manuscript, efforts are underway to formulate Anna University's budget for 2023 and allocate financial resources accordingly. This entails a meticulous review of past expenditures to inform budget allocations for the upcoming year across various departments and centers. The allocation process involves personal consultations with department heads and central directors to ascertain their funding needs and ensure accurate distribution.

Efficient collaboration between Directors and Department heads is crucial, with strategic planning serving as the cornerstone of this endeavour. They must devise comprehensive plans outlining anticipated fund utilization, prepare procurement quotations, and obtain Vice-Chancellor's approval through committee submission.

The responsibility lies squarely on department heads and central directors to reconcile divergent committee opinions and secure awaited funds. As Dr. A.P.J. Abdul Kalam eloquently stated in his autobiography "The Wings of Fire," finance serves as an invaluable catalyst, with adequate funding enabling teams to accomplish eighty percent of their objectives, leaving only the remaining twenty percent to diligent effort.

Reflecting on my tenure as Deputy Director at IQAC, these insights underscore the significance of meticulous planning and resource management in driving organizational success.

Crystallize your thinking

The art of translating thoughts into tangible outcomes is a rare skill possessed by a select few. Within the academic realm, many individuals translate their research insights into scholarly papers, yet only a handful possess the exceptional ability to bridge the gap between academic findings and practical applications. One such remarkable individual who has captivated my attention is Professor Senthil Kumar.

With a master's degree in avionics and a bachelor's degree in electrical engineering, Professor Senthil Kumar embarked on his journey at Anna University as an Assistant Professor in 2004. His prowess in Drone-based Unmanned

Aerial Vehicles, coupled with his adeptness in research and laboratory practices, has elevated Anna University's standing in the realm of Drone technology. Recognizing his significant contributions, the Government of Tamil Nadu has extended substantial financial support and bestowed upon him the prestigious APJ Abdul Kalam Award.

To further the advancement of Drone technology, the Tamil Nadu government, in collaboration with Anna University, established the "Drone Corporation," marking a pioneering effort in India. This ground-breaking initiative signifies the first instance of a state-government partnership with a university to drive technological innovation. Through this partnership, Anna University and the Government of Tamil Nadu are aligning with the principles of Education Policy 4.0, propelling the state towards technological advancement and academic excellence.

Want to know a secret?

Have you ever wondered about the core principle that propels Professor K. Senthil Kumar's endeavours? I once inquired, and with a smile, he responded, "Teamwork." Indeed, his assertion holds true. His team is expansive, comprising individuals with diverse talents and expertise. Within this multifaceted ensemble, you'll encounter individual's adept at piloting aircraft, others with deep expertise in electronics, and yet more skilled in the integration of Drone Technology. It's a dynamic team brimming with vitality, driven by a collective spirit of achievement. Regardless of the task at hand, you'll always find a palpable sense of enthusiasm permeating through this team.

The myriad accomplishments of Professor Senthil Kumar didn't materialize overnight through some magical feat.

Rather, they are the culmination of twelve years of relentless dedication and collaborative effort. I vividly recall our initial encounter eleven years ago, when I first crossed paths with him as a post-graduate student in my classroom.

Professor Senthil Kumar's passion for Drones was palpable from the moment he spoke his first word in our classroom: "Drones." For nearly an hour, he passionately expounded on their potential applications and future implications. It was an era where reconnaissance aircraft and their components were scarcely available. Undeterred by these challenges, he would embark on arduous journeys to Delhi, traveling in unreserved train coaches to procure unmanned aerial vehicles for the benefit of his students.

Even today, remnants of those early endeavours can be found in the Aerospace Department of the MIT Campus at Anna University. In 2008, Professor Senthil Kumar achieved his first documented success by participating in a Drone competition organized by the Indian Defence Research and Development Organisation (DRDO), where he clinched the third prize. Yet, despite this recognition, he remained unsatisfied, continually striving for greater heights.

Why?

As we reached the third level, an unusual sight unfolded before us: Professor Senthil Kumar, typically composed and unwavering, was visibly restless, his mind consumed by relentless contemplation throughout the night. This marked a stark departure from his usual demeanour, leaving us taken aback.

Throughout the tournament, our team had found solace and sanctuary within the confines of the avionics laboratory, where we spent countless hours tirelessly pursuing our goals. Even after the awards ceremony, this refuge remained our haven. While the rest of us succumbed to exhaustion following the competition, Professor Senthil Kumar alone grappled with insomnia, driven by an unyielding determination to unearth the root cause of our setback.

In a moment of clarity, amidst the dim glow of laboratory lights, he made a breakthrough discovery: the interference of video transmitter harmonics waves with GPS signals had led to our falter on the third level. With this revelation, he finally allowed himself the luxury of peaceful slumber.

From that pivotal moment onward, Professor Senthil Kumar emerged as an indomitable force in every competition he entered. His unwavering resolve and methodical approach to analysing failures served as a beacon of inspiration. Indeed, he exemplifies how failures fail to plague those who dissect them with precision, illuminating the path to success through diligent analysis.

Charm with Leadership

One of the primary factors that attract individuals to a specific company is its leadership. Renowned leadership expert and motivational author Brian Tracy underscores the significance of leadership in his writings. In his book on the subject, Tracy offers two definitions of leadership that particularly resonate with me.

Firstly, he describes leadership as "the capacity to elicit exceptional outcomes from ordinary individuals." This definition encapsulates the transformative power of effective leadership, highlighting its ability to unlock hidden potential and drive remarkable achievements.

Secondly, Tracy characterizes leadership as "a concerted effort to empower individuals to lead themselves." This definition underscores the role of leadership in fostering self-reliance and intrinsic motivation among team members, thereby cultivating a culture of autonomy and empowerment.

These definitions succinctly capture the essence of leadership, emphasizing its role in galvanizing teams towards shared goals and fostering personal and professional growth.

The allure for young talent to join the Japanese electronics giant Sony stemmed from its distinctive approach to leadership and innovation. Rather than merely catering to existing market demands, Sony pioneered the creation of markets for its products, setting a new paradigm in the industry. Central to this approach was Sony's unwavering commitment to prioritizing the voices and insights of its youthful workforce.

At Sony, young employees were afforded ample opportunities to refine their skills and unleash their unique talents. The company placed a premium on individuality, actively seeking out recruits who possessed distinct capabilities and perspectives. In a departure from conventional hiring practices, Sony often entrusted young hires with roles aligned with their passions and aspirations.

Furthermore, Sony demonstrated its unwavering support for innovation by allocating substantial resources for research and development initiatives, empowering employees to pursue ground-breaking ideas with enthusiasm. This bold strategy yielded dual benefits for the company: firstly, it fostered a culture of continuous learning and skill enhancement among employees, resulting in the creation of world-class technologies and tools. Secondly, it bolstered Sony's reputation as a trailblazer in leadership and innovation, attracting top talent eager to contribute to the company's vision.

Two types of leaders

In my view, leadership based solely on position, wealth, and authority is inherently fleeting. Lasting leadership emerges when individuals willingly choose to follow someone, recognizing their qualities and vision. True leaders are those who inspire trust and loyalty among their followers, not those who simply wield power.

In leading organizations effectively, it's essential to have two distinct types of leaders. One type collaborates with others, harnessing collective efforts to achieve common goals. The other type brings fresh perspectives and innovative approaches to problem-solving, driving progress through unconventional means.

Identifying the first type of leader within an organization is relatively straightforward, as their collaborative nature and active involvement are readily apparent. However, recognizing leaders of the second type requires significant effort and discernment. These individuals often shy away from traditional leadership roles and may not actively seek recognition.

Integrating such individuals into leadership positions can yield transformative results, as their unique insights and approaches can unlock untapped potential and translate goals into tangible achievements. Yet, the process of identifying and empowering these unconventional leaders presents a considerable challenge, demanding perseverance and insight.

Avoid forming opinions about others

Professor Sethuraman stands out among the many leaders I've encountered in my career. He is a highly respected expert in accreditation processes like NAAC, NRA, and NIR ranking. Our first meeting occurred during the 2012 NAAC review process. One of the department heads unexpectedly removed a gun from his possession before the presentation began. In that way, he demonstrated his wealth of experience and decisive nature that day. It was an unforgettable experience for me, from the first time I saw him in person to his calming presence during the head of the department's outburst. In 2023, NAAC appointed a peer team to review Anna University. I was entrusted with the task of accompanying Professor Sethuraman, who was part of the peer team. Despite my initial reservations, meeting him in person completely changed my perception of him.

He's a delight to engage with socially, showing genuine care and empathy for those around him. He consistently offers words of encouragement, uplifting others whenever the chance arises. Even small steps towards leadership receive his attentive and appreciative support. His presence exudes positivity, and his smile alone serves as a beacon of encouragement for new ventures and achievements. Working alongside him feels like a divine opportunity bestowed upon me. Though our time together was brief, our bond resembled that of a father and son, albeit strained. Our discussions spanned topics from the essence of leadership to the boundless potential of human minds, leaving me inspired by his forward-thinking insights on future human development.

Time management

Effective time management is paramount in leadership. It's your responsibility to articulate your ideas and expectations to your team within designated timeframes, reflecting your ethical commitment. Failure to do so implies a misalignment with your own directives. Whether addressing small groups or large audiences, prioritize punctuality. Begin by outlining your key points and organizing them sequentially. Allocate time slots accordingly, and engage in rehearsals or mock exercises at least twice before any presentation. This proactive approach will significantly enhance your journey toward mastering time management skills.

Have you observed how, during critical moments, some leaders inadvertently convey something other than their intended message? This serves as a prime example of poor time management and planning. As you commence your speech, bear in mind the countless leaders and team members attentively observing someone of your stature. Strive to articulate your points with utmost clarity, ensuring your focus remains aligned with the key messages you aim to convey.

Ensuring a seamless leadership shift for continued success

Have you experienced the luxury of traveling in high-end cars? They boast such elegant designs that neither the engine nor the vehicle's vibrations are perceptible. Their smooth operation makes the journey seamless, almost imperceptible. Conversely, have you ever ridden in autos or tractors? Their journey can be rather discomforting, as the engine vibrations tend to unsettle passengers. In mechanical engines, motion is generated by the controlled explosion of fuel, such as petrol or diesel, within a chamber. This energy is then harnessed by a crankshaft, converting the piston's upward and downward movements into mechanical energy to propel the vehicle forward. Heavy vehicles often feature multiple piston systems attached to crankshafts, resulting in noticeable vibrations with each explosion. While these controlled explosions occur at regular intervals to conserve fuel, they also contribute to the vibrations experienced in autos and tractors. To mitigate this, high-end luxury cars employ a technique called the "Pilot Burn," a deliberate third explosion introduced between two primary blasts to minimize vibrations. Similarly, in the realm of leadership transitions, it's crucial to ensure a seamless handover that doesn't disrupt employees or operations. This necessitates the careful selection and training of future leaders well in advance.

A leader should be prepared for a variety of meetings, including departmental gatherings. From what I have observed, many companies lack this conducive atmosphere. When inexperienced leaders lacking administrative training and field experience assume roles, they often start from square one. This can result in periods of chaos, stagnation, and administrative disarray. Here, experience refers not to tenure within the company but rather to proficiency in departmental administration and leadership management.

****

7. Seek Guidance

In leadership, the challenges you encounter and the context in which they arise can often diverge. The essence of leadership lies in a perpetual learning journey, where one must be equipped to confront these challenges at every turn, minute by minute. Occasionally, circumstances may demand insights, wisdom, and interventions from leaders who have excelled in different domains. Being open to adopting best practices from diverse teams is crucial not only for fostering a healthy work environment but also for enhancing overall company productivity.

During the final testing phase, the "Prithvi" surface-to-surface missile, developed by the Defence Research and Development Organisation (DRDO), encountered defects in its control software, presenting a seemingly insurmountable challenge. Lt. Gen. VJ Sundaram, the project's Director-General, and Dr. Abdul Kalam, the Director of the project, immediately turned to the Indian Space Research Organisation (ISRO) for assistance in rectifying the software deficiencies. Their collaborative efforts resulted in a historic milestone as the Prithvi missile successfully soared into space on February 25, 1988. This event stands as a compelling testament to the transformative power of collective leadership, shared experiences, and collaborative endeavours in achieving significant milestones.

"The counsel and leadership of others, along with their invaluable experiences, will steer and support us as we navigate our journey"

Productivity vs. Human Mind

When discussing productivity, we are essentially delving into the realm of human cognition, making it imperative to do so. Productivity and the human mind share a direct correlation. Want to enhance productivity within your workplace? It's imperative to delve into the myriad intricacies of the human psyche. Merely operating under stress may marginally impact productivity; however, it's crucial to recognize that stress alone doesn't unveil one's full potential. Teams driven by motivation and adept at handling crises seldom display their optimal performance. They may adopt a mindset where fulfilling duties suffices, neglecting the potential for broader contributions. Such an environment doesn't foster mutual benefit between the team and management. While productivity may surge during challenging times, it often complicates tasks rather than simplifying them. Adequate rest and downtime are essential for teams to navigate such predicaments successfully. It falls upon the Team Leader to undertake all necessary measures to steer the team effectively through such situations.

Effective management

Instead of solely relying on sheer effort, embracing strategic endeavours known as "smart work" greatly fosters the advancement of both the team and the company. To attain maximal productivity with fewer resources, teams must possess adequate expertise, or team leaders should equip their teams accordingly. This involves periodically offering essential training and workshop sessions to the team. Additionally, team members should be incentivized to participate in mindfulness and leadership courses as needed. Such proactive measures by the leader will reshape the committee and optimize its operations.

Step away for a moment

Feeling stuck in a rut with your work? Finding it frustrating? It might be time for a break. And not just any break - a proper, complete leave. Step away from your responsibilities temporarily. Put your laptops away, stash your mobile phones, and head back to your hometown. Reconnect with your family - spend quality time with your parents and loved ones. Embark on a journey to uncharted territories, immersing yourself in new experiences. This freshness will invigorate your mind, fostering joy and offering a golden chance to rediscover peace and replenish your energy. Upon your return, you'll perceive a positive transformation within yourself, brimming with renewed enthusiasm to tackle your tasks. Success will naturally ensue.

****

8. Paragons of Leadership Excellence

Commencing with the circulars you dispatch as a leader, individuals scrutinize every aspect of your communication - from the content of your messages to your ideas, speeches, eloquence, demeanour, attitudes, and planning. As a leader, you conscientiously evaluate your conduct. If deemed appropriate, others seek to emulate it; otherwise, it invites critique. Your conduct serves as the linchpin of your success, shaping the behavior of both your team and your organization. Regarding conduct, setting a compelling example as a team leader is paramount; only then will your team wholeheartedly rally behind you. They will seek to glean insights and knowledge from your actions. Let's explore some key traits that people closely observe in their leaders and aspire to emulate.

Act with integrity

As a leader, integrity is paramount—avoid deceit, cheating, or taking shortcuts. Any breach of trust erodes the foundation upon which your team relies. Embrace accountability for the repercussions of your decisions. While it may be tempting to shift blame onto others, remember, your subordinates may remain silent out of fear of repercussions, yet they discern the truth. Baseless accusations and unjust actions tarnish your reputation. Dishonest conduct sets a detrimental precedent for your team's behavior. Beware of the ripple effect: when leaders engage in deception, it can foster a culture of dishonesty throughout the organization, from top to bottom, leading to its eventual downfall.

Maintain a professional demeanour

Embrace a mindset conducive to shaping your aspirations. It's the perspective of viewing success and failure with equanimity that propels ordinary employees into adept leaders. Neither setbacks nor failures immobilize leaders; instead, they use them as stepping stones for growth. With each success and failure, they refine their skills, learning valuable lessons along the way. Dynamic leaders exude positivity, manifesting energy in their thoughts, words, and deeds. Consequently, they garner the full confidence of their peers, steering a company away from failure and toward success. Such actions serve as potent motivators for leaders to continuously improve. Cultivating the right mindset is crucial for steering toward success.

Foster a culture of mutual respect

Your conduct towards others sets the tone for how your team and organization interact with others. As a leader, it's imperative to exemplify the right mindset at all times. One of your primary responsibilities as a team leader is to treat your employees with respect. Whether they hold a higher or lower position, everyone deserves to be treated with dignity. Incorporate respectful language into your interactions and emphasize its importance to your team members. Over time, this respectful demeanour will become the standard within your team. Since employees convey approximately 80 percent of their communication to customers, ensure that the language used is positive and adds value to the interaction.

Exemplify good habits

Every action you take is closely observed by all employees within your company. Exceptional leaders demonstrate diligence and commitment by putting in long hours of hard work. This dedication serves as a motivating force for all employees to emulate. When leaders arrive early and work tirelessly, their employees are inspired to follow suit. Distinguished leaders captivate their employees through their exemplary actions, which significantly influence the behavior of the workforce. Hence, it's crucial for leaders to set a positive example and embody commendable habits.

Relinquish narrow-mindedness and the inclination to criticize

Group leaders and their members must recognize that we are perpetually engaged in a pursuit for a greater purpose, and our actions serve as the catalyst for significant change. It's imperative to understand that neither short-sightedness nor self-interest should overshadow the group's productivity and the company's advancement. A crucial aspect of effective managerial skills involves overcoming criticism. Critics, characterized by their negativity, incessantly point out flaws without acknowledging diligent efforts. They dwell on what could have been done differently, often dismissing your endeavours as futile. Engaging with them proves fruitless; explanations fall on deaf ears as they persist in fault-finding. Like a frog in a well, they spread negativity to those around them. If you encounter such individuals, it's advisable to disengage. Refrain from squandering your valuable energy on futile conversations.

As the proverb goes, "a frog will spoil itself with its own mouth"; they undermine their own dignity and hinder success in life. Negative thoughts possess the potential to influence not just you but also those in your vicinity. However, negative thoughts are inherent in human nature. Yet, with positive thinking, good habits, and exposure to inspiring literature and affirmations, you can transform negativity into positivity. Give it a shot.

Act with purpose

Begin by organizing your objectives and aspirations. Determine today where you envision yourself in five years' time, and commence the necessary actions to realize those ambitions starting now. Individuals devoid of clear goals struggle to achieve success in any endeavour. History's most influential leaders propel themselves forward through exemplary deeds, meticulously crafting plans and taking decisive actions to attain their objectives. Ultimately, they streamline their goals, rallying the entire team behind a shared vision. As leaders and employees align towards a common goal, a palpable sense of enthusiasm pervades, portraying them as resolute and committed individuals.

Hard work

Success presents a formidable challenge to all, yet leaders pave the way for its attainment through sheer dedication. If you've achieved success through hard work, you embody the essence of great leadership. Within you lie the essential qualities requisite for leadership, including strategic planning, unwavering perseverance, and self-motivation. Endeavor to harness these qualities within yourself. Exceptional leaders consistently toil, relentlessly seeking avenues to enhance efficiency. They eagerly adopt innovative approaches whenever opportunity arises. I've observed some leaders who rise early each morning, arriving at the office ahead of schedule and departing only after everyone else has left. Their capital lies in the additional time they invest daily, a practice that significantly boosts their productivity. Are you striving to institute positive change within your office and company? Rely steadfastly on hard work; it serves as a solid cornerstone for transformation, benefiting both you and those around you.

****

9. Step into Leadership

Alexander and Aristotle

When discussing leadership, allow me to share a captivating anecdote from the life of Alexander the Great. On a certain day, Aristotle gathered all his students, including Alexander, for a discussion. Addressing them, Aristotle posed a thought-provoking question: "If any of you were to ascend to the throne, what principles would govern your rule?"

Enthusiastically, each student offered their vision:

"I would establish a flawless government."

"I'd institute a law exempting citizens from taxes."

"I'd ensure free education for all."

"I'd create widespread employment opportunities."

Amidst these responses, Alexander remained silent, deep in contemplation.

Aristotle then inquired, "And how would you handle challenges that arise?"

"We would seek your guidance directly," the students replied unanimously.

Turning his attention to Alexander, Aristotle awaited his response.

Alexander, with quiet confidence, replied, "I would carefully assess the situation, drawing upon the knowledge and critical thinking skills you've imparted to me through education. Thus equipped, I would make decisions aligned with the nation's best interests"

This resolute answer filled Aristotle with pride, highlighting the depth of Alexander's understanding and his readiness for leadership.

A leader must grasp the context, exercise independent thought, and make decisions aligned with the needs of the people and the team's welfare. This, to me, stands as a cornerstone of effective leadership. The recounted episode from Alexander the Great's life serves as a timeless illustration of how he marshalled a formidable army and exerted influence over diverse regions, underscoring the importance of such leadership qualities.

Ensure the concept is comprehended accurately

Hitler's rise to power in Germany can be attributed to his exceptional oratory prowess. Starting with a measured pace, he gradually intensified his delivery, tailoring his rhetoric to resonate with his audience's sentiments. He skilfully employed emotion when needed, accelerating his cadence and employing commanding body language to captivate his listeners, ultimately reaching a crescendo that left no room for dissent. Initially honing his skills in solitude, Hitler then honed his craft among peers, gradually shedding his inhibitions to address smaller gatherings such as the "Beer Hall" meetings. With each round of applause, his confidence burgeoned. A pivotal moment in Hitler's trajectory was his realization that his forte lay not in painting but in the power of speech. As a leader, effectively conveying your thoughts and ideas to your team is paramount. A true mark of leadership is the ability to articulate concepts clearly and convincingly to one's subordinates.

Do you want to become a great leader?

Studying the biographies of great leaders and their journeys reveals a clear pattern: they adeptly adapt themselves to their circumstances. This insight sheds light on why they garner such admiration and wield such influence over people. Leaders are not born; rather, they evolve in response to the exigencies of their times.

Consider Napoleon's story: it took him approximately two decades to reclaim Corsica, his birthplace. Initially serving as a lieutenant in the French government, he strategized a daring assault on the island. Despite facing formidable odds within the French army, his efforts in Corsica proved futile, leading to his arrest and imprisonment for insurrection against the state. However, leveraging the tumult of the French Revolution, he crafted a comprehensive proposal that impressed the provisional French government, facilitating his reinstatement in the army—this time as a commander.

Through unwavering perseverance, meticulous planning, and a positive approach to adversity, Napoleon achieved remarkable success. From conquering Italy, Europe, and Egypt to ascending as the French monarch, his journey exemplifies the essence of leadership. Napoleon's history underscores the transformative power of perseverance, strategic planning, and adept crisis management—a potent trifecta that underscores the potential for achieving extraordinary feats.

The primary task at hand revolves around mental functions

While goals and achievements hold significance, noble successes propel both you and your company toward sustainable growth. These triumphs infuse your mind with joy and vitality. To cultivate happiness, persist in tackling challenging tasks—your ability to overcome them shapes the trajectory of your leadership journey. Easy victories offer little opportunity for skill development. Achievements attained through mere delegation or passive observation lack substance and fail to enhance leadership qualities. True leaders are esteemed for their willingness to roll up their sleeves and dive into the fray. Whether it's Alexander the Great or Napoleon, their credibility stemmed from their willingness to lead from the frontlines, showcasing their valour on the battlefield.

Were you aware of a distinct practice observed in the armies of Alexander the Great, Stalin, and Napoleon? It involved appointing individuals with little or no military background as commanders within their armies.

Why?

They earned recognition through their cognitive abilities, in essence, their strong personalities. They possess the knack for extracting the best performance from their subordinates. Historical accounts affirm that none of these individuals lacking formal military training failed to make a significant impact.

Life and train journey

Summing up life in a single line, it's akin to a captivating train journey. Embrace all its offerings and keep moving forward. It's human nature to anticipate finding something specific at the next station, only to discover something entirely different. Accepting these unexpected turns and persisting on our life journey is vital. When opportunities arise, seize them to lead a fulfilling life. Along the way, some may accompany us until the journey's end, while others depart at their designated stops. Dwelling on such transitions inhibits progress to the next stage of life. Letting go and moving forward are essential facets of human existence. Often, we fret over unfulfilled desires, but it's crucial to accept them gracefully and continue our journey, recognizing our strengths and appreciating what we have. Moreover, it's essential to keep striving to enhance our talents further.

Stay away from negative-minded people

Individuals harbouring negative thoughts possess a cunning ability to manipulate and influence others easily. It's advisable to distance yourself from them temporarily, as they can swiftly taint your positive mindset with negativity. Avoid those who habitually criticize and spread pessimism about management and circumstances. If you encounter such individuals, excuse yourself by citing work obligations. These negative-minded individuals offer no benefit to the organization; they thrive in creating a toxic environment surrounded by a compliant audience. They continuously propagate negativity, often frequenting places like canteens and intersections to disseminate their harmful thoughts. Beware of their deceptive tactics; their sweet talk serves no purpose in enhancing your well-being or productivity in the workspace.

****

10. Radiate Enthusiasm

At times, the demands of our work may leave us feeling overwhelmed and drained of enthusiasm. During such moments, it's essential to take a comprehensive break from our responsibilities. Ensure you get ample rest, cultivate a tranquil mindset, and indulge in rejuvenating activities, such as taking refreshing baths or strolls in nearby parks or temples. Treat yourself to your favourite meals and prioritize physical exercise or morning walks to invigorate your body and mind. Engage with others warmly, offering genuine inquiries about their well-being, as this fosters increased creativity and self-respect. By doing so, you can dispel any misconceptions others may have about you and reignite your enthusiasm, enabling you to tackle tasks with renewed vigour and energy.

Stay healthy

Prioritize your well-being to ensure optimal physical health and vitality. Despite busy schedules, refrain from skipping breakfast, as it serves as a vital source of energy. Consume a nutritious lunch, focusing on incorporating ample protein into your daily diet. Consider taking a brief nap post-lunch, as studies show it can significantly boost energy levels. Aim to complete dinner before 7 p.m., as consuming food after this time may lead to unnecessary weight gain, particularly when stressed. Minimize exposure to stressors, as stress is a primary contributor to obesity. Strive to compartmentalize work-related concerns and leave them at the office, avoiding comparisons with personal life. Even if acquaintances engage in office-related tasks at home, resist the urge to follow suit, as this detracts from both personal and professional progress. Cherish every moment spent with family, recognizing its irreplaceable value. Refrain from sacrificing these precious moments for any reason or circumstance.

Impetus for productivity

Do you ever wonder why the Indian Space Research Organisation (ISRO) continues to achieve remarkable feats today?

Professor Satish Dhawan assumed leadership of the Indian space mission following the passing of Prof Vikram Sarabhai, often hailed as the father of the Indian space movement. Dhawan observed a dedicated workforce, with many ISRO staff working tirelessly beyond regular hours. Upon investigation, he discovered that labs remained operational until midnight, sometimes with scientists working through the night.

While he acknowledged the importance of dedication to national progress, Dhawan recognized the necessity of balance. He understood that without adequate rest, personal happiness, familial care, and focus, achieving comprehensive goals would remain elusive. Thus, Prof. Dhawan introduced a revolutionary approach at ISRO.

Regardless of the task's urgency, Dhawan mandated that no scientist work beyond 5 p.m. Lab doors would promptly close at this hour. After 5 p.m., scientists were to shed their scientific attire and assume the mantle of family caretaker, spending quality time with their loved ones as devoted parents, spouses, and children.

Professor Satish Dhawan's innovative approach brought about a transformative shift within the Indian Space Research Organisation and laid the groundwork for the organization's subsequent achievements.

True fulfillment in both personal and professional life arises when one finds joy in giving. Visionary leaders like Prof. Dhawan exemplify this principle, recognizing its profound impact on productivity. This ethos remains ingrained within ISRO, a testament to its enduring effectiveness.

Amidst the perpetual demands of work, it's crucial to carve out moments for oneself. These noble pursuits form the bedrock of happiness and serve as catalysts for heightened productivity. Ultimately, the onus lies on individuals to fulfil their tasks and obligations, leveraging the support of colleagues and assistants while taking full responsibility for their actions.

Clarity in defining objectives and charting a course of action facilitates the accomplishment of challenging tasks. Dedication to meeting deadlines and fulfilling commitments is paramount in leadership. Leaders prioritize results over excuses, understanding that the incessant pursuit of reasons only hinders progress. Excelling in leadership demands a steadfast commitment to completing tasks and obligations punctually, forsaking the inclination to justify shortcomings. Embracing this ethos fosters continual growth and success in leadership endeavours.

Thumb rule of leadership

Don't allow yourself to be stifled by management; instead, take charge of the situation. Management can often discourage you, but when you assert control, you can harness the myriad ideas swirling in your mind. Superficial approaches may obscure the truth of management's capabilities, but closer examination reveals its true potential. Occasionally, working under management may conceal your talents, denying you recognition and rights. In such instances, maintaining a positive mindset is a form of self-motivation.

Navigating through challenging times can make it difficult to adhere to these principles. Therefore, strive to establish an environment where you influence management rather than being subjugated by it. This not only showcases your capabilities but also allows you to translate your ideas into action effectively.

Make alternative plans

Entrusting administration to incompetent individuals can unravel your hard work in mere moments. It's crucial to have contingency plans in place to ensure effective management. When management veers off course, it's imperative to implement these backup strategies. Pre-select capable leaders who can steer your management and company towards growth. Provide them with comprehensive training, strategies, and managerial insights in advance.

A visionary leader always anticipates the future, meticulously planning the path forward to facilitate collective success. Napoleon, the revered figure renowned for shaping history, didn't solely rely on battlefield victories for his triumphs. In times of adversity, alternative plans were meticulously crafted in advance, outlining directives for his army commanders. Napoleon's success was predicated on his adeptness at adapting alternative strategies to suit the circumstances, elevating him to legendary status.

Be prepared to accept the responsibilities of leadership

Do you aspire to elevate your leadership prowess? Begin by embracing leadership responsibilities wholeheartedly. Cultivate unwavering confidence in your ability to guide a remarkable team towards success. Enhance your leadership acumen by diligently adhering to these seven pivotal responsibilities outlined below. This approach is universally applicable, fostering the growth and advancement of any organization.

1. Set goals and try to achieve them

Begin by establishing both personal and team objectives that align with your aspirations. Craft a strategic roadmap outlining the steps necessary to accomplish these goals. Break down significant efforts into manageable milestones, creating a clear trajectory for success. Exceptional leaders possess a keen understanding of their organization's strengths, weaknesses, and past achievements. With a keen eye on profitability and continuous improvement, strategize and execute initiatives aimed at enhancing business outcomes and achieving set objectives. Success will naturally follow your diligent efforts.

2. Make innovative efforts

Break free from the confines of conventional practices entrenched within your company's culture for years. Embrace innovative initiatives that have the potential to exponentially expand your customer base. In the realm of sales, equip your employees with contemporary digital marketing strategies to enhance outreach and engagement. Embrace modern infrastructure and cutting-edge technologies within your organization, infusing a sense of vitality and dynamism. These endeavours not only invigorate your workforce but also propel your company towards the realization of its overarching objectives.

3. Problems Find out and try to get rid of it

Life's journey is incomplete without encountering challenges along the way; they are an intrinsic part of the human experience. No company traverses its path without encountering obstacles enroute to its goals. Each unattained goal in life represents an unresolved challenge awaiting resolution. These challenges manifest themselves periodically, demanding our attention and action.

Begin by cataloguing the issues plaguing your organization, categorizing them based on their solvability. Address the easily soluble problems within your purview as a priority. As you tackle these challenges head-on, you'll notice that seemingly insurmountable obstacles begin to unravel one by one.

Remember, no challenge is insurmountable; the key lies in addressing the simpler problems first. By swiftly resolving these, you pave the way for overcoming more complex issues.

4. Prioritize tasks requiring immediate attention

Exceptional leaders meticulously categorize their actions, distinguishing between those requiring immediate attention and those suitable for later action. They prioritize tasks necessitating immediate completion, swiftly taking steps to address them without delay. Recognizing the significance and potential consequences of prompt action, they effectively communicate the benefits to both the company and its employees. By expeditiously attending to critical tasks, they streamline workflows and facilitate smoother operations, ultimately fostering success.

5. Try to be a role model for others

Captivate your employees and colleagues with your conduct. Your team observes your every move as a leader, eager to mirror your demeanour, resilience, and character. They are inclined to emulate your positive actions and behaviours. As an exemplary leader, it is imperative to elevate yourself and endeavour to enhance the well-being of those in your sphere. This proactive approach allows you to lead by example, inspiring others to follow suit.

6. Ignite inspiration in others to join your journey

As a leader, ensure that your team comprehends the rationale behind every decision and its implications. They are the frontline warriors, driving your company's progress and prosperity. It's vital for your employees to grasp how their contributions fuel the company's advancement. Empowered by understanding, their actions transcend mere tasks, imbued with renewed vigour and creative impetus. Do you aspire to inspire your team? Cultivate a practice of transparency and clarity in your leadership, investing in moments of insight and collaboration. This not only enhances your leadership acumen but also garners trust and allegiance from your employees. Upholding this approach will foster a culture of commitment and enthusiasm within your team, propelling them to excel under your guidance.

7. Accumulate success

The company anticipates success solely from an exceptional leader, devoid of any expectation for failures or excuses. Instead, the focus lies on meticulously analysing the root cause of failure and transforming it into a triumph of leadership. This seventh responsibility outweighs the preceding six in its significance for leadership. To thrive in leadership, prioritize the accumulation of successes.

****

11. Be Ready to Assume Responsibility

Leaders recognize that they bear sole accountability for the outcomes of their actions. They eschew the temptation to evade responsibility through excuses or justifications for errors. Whether favourable or unfavourable, triumphant or disappointing, leaders must be poised to embrace the repercussions of their decisions. Embracing accountability stands as the paramount stride towards refining leadership acumen and propelling oneself towards evolutionary advancement in leadership prowess.

Form a team of achievers

Leadership isn't an inherent trait; rather, it's a product of deliberate self-cultivation. Leaders diligently mould their ideas into reality through persistent effort. To ascend to the pinnacle of leadership, cultivate a dynamic and fervent group, fostering proximity to it. This will elevate your image as a triumphant leader and an authority in leadership. Furthermore, handpick team members who collaborate harmoniously, united in the pursuit of greatness, and actively engage them in your endeavors. Having assembled a winning team, refine your leadership prowess by meticulously attending to the following seven aspects.

1. Connect the best with you

Whether it be Alexander, famed for his triumphs, or Napoleon the Great, they both opted for elite individuals as their commanders, keeping them close. The calibre of a leader can be discerned from the actions of their subordinates. Exceptional leaders consistently enlist individuals of superior ability to serve under them, while ineffectual leaders gravitate towards those of lesser competence. Select individuals who surpass your own capabilities and foster a connection with your team to elevate your strengths.

2. Engage in training and planning work for the development of the team

To ensure optimal team performance, furnish the necessary training and infrastructure. What are the management's expectations, and how can you facilitate administrative progress? Facilitate mutual comprehension by elucidating the methodology to both parties. As a leader, you serve as a conduit between management and employees, endeavouring to align team objectives with company expectations. With transparent communication and effective leadership, the company will persist on its trajectory of success.

3. Planning and its importance

Emphasize the importance of relying on credible information and ensuring its accessibility. Trustworthy data forms the foundation of effective decision-making, never veering from truthfulness. Mere accumulation of information or assumption won't suffice; precision is pivotal for strategic planning. Allocate ample attention to the planning phase of any endeavour, as evidenced by a study from a reputable UK firm suggesting it consumes a significant portion of time. Success hinges on meticulous planning, illustrated by Britain's ability to intercept clandestine communications during World War II, underscoring the significance of thorough information gathering prior to strategic planning for continued success.

Formulate alternate strategies

If things don't unfold as anticipated, refrain from devising and executing new plans hastily. The constraints of the moment might hinder your ability to formulate and implement a superior strategy compared to what was previously devised. Doing so could compound your failure. Instead, incorporate contingency plans into your initial planning process wherever feasible. History recalls how British general Wellington, facing Napoleon at the renowned Waterloo battlefield, prevailed over the adversary through the implementation of alternative strategies.

4. Division of labour

Leverage task delegation as a means to highlight the excellence within your organization. For instance, assigning a complex project to a team member who has shown potential in that area can lead to remarkable results. This approach not only identifies individuals with untapped talent but also fosters their growth and development. By distributing workload among team members, you foster cohesion and collective progress toward shared objectives. Moreover, this approach affords your team exposure to diverse skills, nurturing leadership attributes like collaboration and unity among team members.

5. Ability to weed out the ineligible

The longer you retain unfit individuals in positions of responsibility, the more apparent it becomes to others that you lack discernment as a leader. If someone selected for a role fails to perform adequately, offer guidance and support, providing opportunities for improvement through training and mentoring. Should their performance continue to fall short, termination may be necessary. Allowing unqualified individuals to remain in their roles perpetuates a false narrative that incompetence is tolerated within the company. It's imperative to recognize that such leniency can ultimately undermine the company's integrity and erode trust in its leadership, leading to potential downfall.

6. Better exchange of ideas

When analysing the success stories of leading companies, one common factor emerges: effective communication. Strong communication practices propel management towards growth and development, while poor communication yields negative outcomes. Transparency in exchanging ideas is crucial within organizations and their management structures.

By emphasizing the role of every employee in initiating harmonious interactions, we set the foundation for utilizing communication to analyse organizational tasks. Effective communication can showcase collective impact and foster dynamic processes within the organization, making each employee feel valued and integral to the company's operations. "Effective idea exchange is paramount during collaborative actions and planning processes"

7. The ultimate objective is to achieve optimal results

Your steadfast dedication is validated solely through exemplary results. Your unwavering commitment to delivering excellence to your company serves as a source of inspiration for both yourself and your team, propelling you towards countless achievements. Occasionally, even minor triumphs play a pivotal role in attaining optimal outcomes. This is why leaders frequently emphasize the significance of success and winning.

8. Focus on cultivating qualities that you do not posses

Recognize your existing capabilities and strive to enhance them, advancing your leadership position. Emphasize honing qualities that may currently be lacking in your skill set. By dedicating focus to these new attributes, you embark on a journey of continuous learning and substantial productivity improvement. By giving these areas extra attention, you can cultivate expertise and emerge victorious. Begin by identifying the specific qualities you wish to develop and seek insights from those proficient in those areas. Formulate a plan to integrate these qualities into your repertoire and take proactive steps towards implementation. Within a short span of time, you will notice significant improvements in your actions and effectiveness.

Consider the example of Thyagarajan, a former professor & dean renowned for his expertise in documenting university events. His extensive leadership experience is evident in his multifaceted activities, with comprehensive knowledge readily accessible to him. During NAAC 2023, he observed and pointed out my typing skills were not optimized, potentially hindering my productivity. His advice to focus on improving my typing proficiency proved invaluable, leading to a significant boost in my productivity. Thanks to Professor Thyagarajan for his keen observation and guidance.

As a leader, you're not obligated to adopt every suggestion, but by selectively developing key qualities, you can catalyse profound transformations in your leadership capabilities. This empowers you to choose the areas you want to focus on for your personal growth. Bear in mind the following three guidelines to upgrade yourself.

i) It does not matter where you came from

What's crucial is the path you're headed, not your origin. Your aspirations and the steps you take to realize them shape your success and character. Each stride you make, blending current thought with future envisioning, is a building block for your character.

ii) If you want to specialize in leadership, you need to tweak yourself first

Avoid constructing imaginary barriers around yourself and confining your journey within them. The world is expansive, welcoming countless individuals like yourself with open arms. Remain open to traveling alongside others, listening to their perspectives, and valuing their input. Earning their trust is a crucial responsibility in leadership. Once you've garnered the trust of your colleagues, you can swiftly accomplish your intended objectives.

iii) Acquire the leadership traits essential for your success

You become the embodiment of your aspirations. Begin by cultivating unwavering confidence in your ability to attain any desired level. This self-assurance serves as the bedrock upon which you'll build your journey towards greater heights in the days ahead. With a solid foundation in place, you'll persistently uphold the efforts and principles you've set forth. Therefore, establish a sturdy groundwork for your leadership qualities, ensuring that you embody the leadership traits you seek to attain.

9. Exemplify effective leadership

A leader relentlessly strives for self-improvement with each passing moment, tirelessly pursuing growth. Embodying the four characteristics outlined below, you can continually augment your leadership prowess through unwavering dedication and persistent effort.

i) Overdo a handful of tasks

Consistently engage in actions tailored to your preferences, ones that lead to personal success. These endeavours cultivate positive and creative energies, fostering clarity of thought. Concrete actions not only embody your ideas but also drive notable transformations in your leadership style.

ii) Reduce the frequency of unnecessary tasks

Avoid engaging in unnecessary actions that not only consume your valuable time but also dull your skills and detract from your innate leadership qualities. Steer clear of tasks that serve as mere distractions and instead focus on activities that contribute meaningfully to your growth and development as a leader.

iii) Immediately execute tasks that are necessary but currently neglected

Begin by identifying the essential skills required for effective leadership and actively pursue activities aimed at honing them. Embrace the process of self-discovery and shed any preconceived notions, as it's your distinct abilities that will serve you best when the occasion demands. Prioritize the cultivation of individuality, as it is the cornerstone of superior leadership.

iv) Eliminate time-wasting activities promptly

Steer clear of frivolous pursuits and idle chatter altogether. As a leader, pinpoint the factors that side-track you from your objectives and concentrate on corrective actions. Compile a list of obstacles hindering your leadership and goal achievement. Systematically remove these impediments. Assess your actions through the lens of your objectives. You'll discover that certain tasks once deemed significant have now become trivial.

10. Simple ways to foster collaboration

Elevate your leadership by fostering coordinated cooperation, as it is this collaboration that truly empowers you. Below are key strategies for leveraging power through collaboration, which we will explore in detail.

Firstly, identify key individuals who can support your leadership goals and cultivate strong relationships with them. Demonstrate genuine appreciation for their contributions and acknowledge their unique qualities. Highlight how their actions have indirectly benefited you and take proactive steps to assist them whenever possible, without expecting anything in return. Building genuine connections based on mutual respect and support is essential for fostering lasting friendships.

Secondly, prioritize dedicating time to nurturing these relationships amidst your busy schedule. Set aside time to connect with these individuals, recognizing that these relationships are invaluable assets for your leadership journey.

Lastly, make a concerted effort to enhance and maintain these valuable relationships. Remember important dates such as birthdays and anniversaries, and make an effort to extend heartfelt congratulations and engage in meaningful conversations. Ensure that you remain present in their thoughts by demonstrating genuine care and interest. Ultimately, the relationships you cultivate with talented individuals will greatly influence the success of your leadership endeavors.

11. Establish a collective of like-minded individuals with mutual agreement

Create a team comprised of individuals aspiring for leadership excellence and those with prior leadership experience. Encourage open sharing of personal and leadership experiences within the group, and actively listen to everyone's perspectives. Endeavor to implement the most valuable advice provided by group members, often finding solutions to long-standing challenges in mere moments. Ensure that this team operates with dual objectives: discussing pre-agreed subjects or questions and addressing current issues. Consider including not only external stakeholders but also employees from your organization as members, facilitating periodic feedback sessions to enhance organizational understanding and address emerging issues.

Dr. A.P.J. Abdul Kalam, former President of India and my senior, exemplified the effectiveness of such a consensus-building approach during the development of various missiles under the Department of Defence and Research's integrated launch programs. Despite initial dissent, his collaborative efforts ultimately united disparate stakeholders towards a common goal, leading to significant advancements in India's defence capabilities.

12. Small little things have the power to transform you into a remarkable achiever

Great achievements are often rooted in the little things. Instead of solely focusing on resolving major issues, prioritize addressing minor concerns, as they frequently hold the key to resolving long-standing challenges. Approximately 95 percent of solutions to significant company issues can be found within these minor details. Start by seeking solutions to major issues within the realm of smaller problems; solutions are often readily available.

Having authority means having individuals who are willing to support and remain loyal to you. These individuals are drawn to your leadership qualities and are motivated to assist you, often because you've helped them in some way, whether directly or indirectly. Your ability to positively impact someone's life without realizing it can attract their support and willingness to help you achieve your goals. When someone excels due to your influence, you gain their cooperation and goodwill. These principles are undeniable. Likability is a crucial factor in shaping your power and influence over others. People naturally gravitate towards leaders they like and are inclined to go above and beyond for them. To become a favourite leader, you must first align yourself with the interests of others and demonstrate genuine care for their well-being. Encourage and showcase their talents, highlight your joint successes, and emphasize that your victories are shared victories. A warm smile, articulate communication, genuine concern, and thoughtful inquiries can establish you as one of them. This is precisely why Netaji Subhas Chandra Bose was embraced as a leader during the Indian freedom struggle, as he stood alongside his people and championed their cause.

13. Be a careful listener

Leaders excel in the art of attentive listening, dedicating approximately 50 to 60 percent of their time to hearing others' viewpoints. From office gatherings to conflict resolution sessions, they actively engage in various meetings, prioritizing the act of listening. Enhancing one's listening skills is achieved through practice and attentiveness. As a leader, it's imperative to discern the underlying meaning behind spoken words. Here are some essential tips to uphold during meetings and conversations, aiming to integrate them into your leadership approach whenever possible.

14. Listen carefully and soberly to the opinions of others

Strive to maintain mental clarity as you engage in conversations. Pay meticulous attention to the speaker's message. Only a small fraction, about 7 percent, of communication is conveyed through words. The majority, 38 percent, is conveyed through voice tone, and a significant 55 percent through body language. Consider a friend who adeptly communicates through nuanced voice tones and expressive body language. By mastering these elements, one can effectively convey their intended message. Hitler's captivating oratory, which reshaped Europe, was renowned for its adept manipulation of these three communication dimensions. His speeches were rich in ideas, infused with dynamic vocal fluctuations, and underscored by powerful body language, effectively conveying emotional depth to his audience. A truly exceptional leader possesses the ability to transmit 100 percent of their ideas to others. To excel in leadership, mastering this method is essential. While initially challenging, with perseverance and dedicated practice, mastery of these skills will become second nature.

15. Pause briefly before responding

Before responding, take a moment to pause and fully absorb the ideas presented. Reflect on them internally, searching for the answer within yourself. Initiate your response only after the speaker has concluded their thoughts. When faced with differing viewpoints, inquire about them and seek clarification. Avoid jumping to conclusions, as your position of authority may inhibit your employees from expressing their opinions freely. Encourage open dialogue and provide your team with the freedom to express themselves fully. Prioritize the perspectives of those directly engaged in the field and cultivate strong relationships with them. Napoleon the Great exemplified this approach by intimately knowing his field workers, understanding their needs, and accommodating their opinions. By fostering such a harmonious atmosphere, he successfully commanded the allegiance of the entire French army.

16. Ask questions to clarify

Asking questions serves as a subtle indication to the speaker that you are attentively monitoring their input, but it must be wielded with care, akin to a double-edged sword. Asking questions indiscriminately risks exposing gaps in your understanding and knowledge. However, strategically asking questions shields you from incorrect assumptions and decisions regarding the speaker's message. Never presume comprehension if clarity is lacking; instead, seek clarification.

Summarizing the points raised by those engaging with you, offering your insights, and repeating them back signals your attentive listening and ensures mutual understanding. Embrace any opportunity for clarification if there's been a misunderstanding, using it as a noble chance to rectify any misconceptions.

17. Listen without interruptions

Listen attentively to all opinions without interruption. Disregard any distractions such as phones or radios to maintain focus. By eliminating distractions, you can fully absorb complete ideas and enhance critical thinking. This attentive listening not only garners the respect and goodwill of the speaker but also facilitates meaningful exchange of ideas.

****

12. Embody the Lifestyle of Leadership

Exceptional leaders exude vibrancy and creativity, embodying leadership in their speech, demeanour, and conduct. They recognize that their actions not only shape their own lives but also drive the growth of their organizations. Proactively, they devise plans and strategies to navigate through future crises and challenges, steadfastly maintaining the mental and physical fortitude needed to overcome adversity. Here are some key steps that exceptional leaders take to inspire growth and development.

Sleep adequately

Prioritize getting 7 to 8 hours of sleep nightly to replenish your physical energy, alleviate fatigue, and invigorate your body for optimal performance. Quality sleep enhances cognitive function and boosts motivation, providing a vital source of inspiration for the challenges ahead. As a leader, maintaining vigilance is paramount, and adequate sleep ensures heightened alertness and a positive demeanour. Minimize activities that disrupt sleep, such as frequenting nightclubs or entertainment venues, to safeguard against compromised actions the following day. Embrace rest as a cornerstone of your well-being, fostering a steadfast mind to greet the opportunities that await.

Embrace solitude and tranquillity as your allies

Transform your workspace to foster a serene and tranquil atmosphere, conducive to enhanced idea exchange. A peaceful environment promotes clear articulation of thoughts and facilitates deep absorption of concepts. Prioritize minimizing smartphone usage and keep distractions like television and radio at bay. Utilize this time for reading or task planning instead. Dedicate at least thirty minutes to an hour to solitude, during which you can reflect on comments and ideas that arise. Compile a list of priority tasks, leveraging this isolated planning time to organize your day and think critically about objectives to be achieved. Embracing solitude in planning cultivates the clarity and creativity essential for effective leadership.

Behave with dignity

As a remarkable leader, embody the essence of a coin, which symbolizes doubling confidence and value, thereby inspiring others to follow. Exercise discernment before accepting responsibilities, ensuring you can lead effectively and honour commitments with integrity. Backing down after accepting a responsibility diminishes your self-assurance; therefore, take the necessary time to deliberate. Uphold the unwavering nature of a coin, avoiding actions that compromise your integrity and diminish your self-worth. Authenticity and truthfulness are essential; resist the temptation to offer false promises that sow hope but lack substance.

Embrace the journey of leadership, even if recognition may be delayed or elusive due to your commitment to integrity. Remain steadfast in your principles, regardless of external pressures or praise-seeking individuals who seek to obscure reality. Avoid flattery and instead prioritize honesty, even in challenging situations where the truth may be difficult to accept. Remember that deceiving others ultimately leads to self-deception, undermining your credibility and moral compass.

Avoid aligning yourself with groups that lack lateral thinking

If you find yourself surrounded by individuals lacking alternative perspectives, it signifies you're headed in the wrong direction. Groups devoid of diverse thinking seldom yield positive outcomes. Dissent fosters innovative thinking, sparking conflicts of opinion that challenge conventional views and pave the way for new perspectives. While consensus may initially appear beneficial for organizational harmony and growth, it stifles innovation and creative thought. Embracing dissenting opinions elevates your own views and actions, often leading to highly favourable outcomes. Therefore, seek out alternative viewpoints and prioritize those who offer dissenting opinions. Their ideas may hold the key to solving previously insurmountable challenges.

Choose to venture jointly

As a leader, prioritize decisions that benefit both you and your employees, fostering an environment where opportunities align with individual skills. Continuously support your team members in honing their abilities, emphasizing the advantages of collective efforts over individual actions. Attribute your successes to collaborative endeavours and their resultant actions.

Reflecting on a noteworthy collaboration at Anna University, The Quacquerelli Simonts, an organization known for its innovative approach, introduced a novel method of promoting sustainability goals, aligned with the United Nations' 17 sustainable development goals. Recognizing the significance of this initiative for global university rankings, Anna University eagerly joined the effort. Under the guidance of Vice-Chancellor Velraj Ramalingam, a dynamic committee comprising seasoned leaders, executives, and newcomers was formed. Professor Ramalingam, renowned for his expertise as a researcher, educator, and motivational speaker, fosters an environment of vibrant ideas and positivity. His penchant for alternative thinking and unconventional problem-solving approaches often yields surprising results.

Thanks to the collective action of the team, exhaustive research on global university practices was conducted, resulting in the development of innovative frameworks tailored for Anna University. This achievement underscores the power of collaborative action; individually, such a feat would have been unattainable. A good leader entrusts their team, continuously encourages their growth, and champions the benefits of collective action. Through their actions and collaborative endeavours, they demonstrate their leadership prowess and inspire others to follow suit.

****

13. Determine your Goals

Once you've defined your goals, meticulously list all the necessary steps to achieve them. Continuously brainstorm and incorporate new ideas that come to mind, ensuring your list is comprehensive. Organize this list in both sequential and prioritized formats for effective planning. A sequential organization system enables you to structure activities according to their required sequence and time frame, facilitating balanced planning and timely task completion. Prioritizing tasks through a priority reading list ensures urgent tasks are addressed promptly, offering a lifeline to companies teetering on the brink of failure.

To accomplish significant goals, break them down into smaller, manageable objectives and take decisive action. However, managing a team may present various challenges. As a team leader, it's your responsibility to resolve issues and steer the team in the right direction. Remember, the 20 percent of tasks on your list typically contribute to 80 percent of your achievements. Therefore, meticulous planning is key to success. Minimize distractions during planning sessions, and regularly review and adapt your plans as needed, especially in the face of obstacles or setbacks. Embrace new information and feedback to refine your plans, knowing that each adjustment propels you closer to remarkable accomplishments.

Goals don't matter; it's your actions that matter

Goals are inherently fluid, subject to change over time, but actions remain steadfast, propelling you steadily forward regardless of shifting objectives. Consider this: today, you may embark on an initiative aiming for a profit of 1000 rupees. Tomorrow, that same endeavour could yield 2000 rupees, and the day after, 5000 rupees. The target evolves, but the actions driving towards it remain constant. Therefore, rather than fixating on fluctuating goals, devote your full attention to the consistent actions that bring these goals to fruition.

Get involved in activities primarily to achieve your goals

Your goals are the driving force behind your actions, igniting enthusiasm and shaping your leadership journey. They provide the direction needed for your efforts to be meaningful. Setting annual goals determines the course of your life, while daily goals pave the way for achieving yearly milestones. Initially daunting, the pursuit of daily objectives becomes ingrained in your routine, transforming into habits that define your attitude and lifestyle.

To progress in life and realize your aspirations, focus on the present moment. Embrace each day with reverence, recognizing its significance in shaping your future successes. Today's endeavours lay the foundation for tomorrow's triumphs, making each step a testament to your future achievements. Embrace failures as valuable lessons learned, acknowledging that they contribute to your growth and eventual success. It is through facing challenges that you accumulate the victories that define your life's journey.

Act swiftly

One of the key advantages contributing to goal achievement is the ability to "get things done quickly," a trait exhibited by only two percent of individuals, as revealed by a recent study. Cultivating the habit of swift task completion propels you along the path of growth, accelerating your progress with each completed endeavour. According to insights gathered from consultations with reputable companies, a staggering 85 percent cited "the ability to promptly initiate and conclude vital tasks" as crucial for advancement. As you hone your capability to swiftly tackle assigned tasks, you'll find yourself encountering exciting new opportunities at every turn.

How can you cultivate this habit of rapid task completion? Simply commit to addressing essential tasks without delay, regardless of the work environment's demands! Embrace the mantra "Do it right away!" and reinforce this mindset through repetition, whether it's twice, twenty times, or a hundred times. With each affirmation, you'll find yourself increasingly motivated to prioritize prompt action, making swift task completion a cornerstone of your daily routine.

Share your time with others

When undertaking tasks that contribute value, it's crucial to differentiate between creative and managerial activities. Attempting to blend these two realms can prove counterproductive. Creative endeavours demand an environment where undivided attention and focused thought reign supreme. Conversely, swift action is imperative for managerial tasks in the office setting. Juggling these distinct actions simultaneously is challenging, if not impossible.

When immersed in creative pursuits, it's essential to create a space conducive to deep concentration. Conversely, office activities necessitate rapid decision-making and execution. To navigate this dichotomy effectively, establish clear boundaries and designate specific times for each type of activity. If creative focus is required, signal your need for solitude with a "do not disturb" sign on your door, or seek out secluded spots within the office environment.

Allocate dedicated time blocks, ideally one to two hours, for engaging in value-added activities such as planning and reporting. By consistently immersing yourself in these endeavours, you will cultivate a culture of focused attention and creativity, ultimately yielding optimal results for the company.

Realize that you are merely the counterpart to others

Dr. David McClelland, a distinguished social psychologist from Harvard University, emphasized that a significant portion, around 95 percent, of your achievements and setbacks are influenced by your social circle. In essence, your aspirations and accomplishments are shaped by the company you keep, echoing the proverbial notion that "a fragrance follows the flower." You find yourself mirroring their habits, from dietary preferences to fashion choices, subconsciously integrating them into your lifestyle. If your current state remains unchanged after five years, it suggests you've been traversing alongside the wrong companions on an erroneous path. Prompt action is imperative to remedy this situation. Two essential steps can aid in this endeavour: reshaping your social connections and immersing yourself in enriching literature. Esteemed author and motivational speaker Jim Ron notably stresses that you become the average of the five individuals you associate with the most.

Apply the thirty-three percent principle to achieve the target

Classify the employees in your workplace into three tiers: lower-level, intermediate, and higher-secondary. The bottom 33 percent of employees often resist cooperation and tend to harbour negative attitudes, undermining your efforts with pessimistic remarks. They drain enthusiasm by dismissing your endeavours as futile. Their stance typically involves impeding progress, both for themselves and others. Conversely, the middle 33 percent of employees exhibit contentment when operations proceed smoothly but adopt a negative stance when faced with disruptions. Finally, the remaining 33 percent of employees persistently champion the company's advancement with unwavering positivity, even amidst adversity. Surrounding yourself with individuals who exemplify such resilience and optimism fosters a similar mindset, influencing your actions accordingly.

****

14. Factors for Motivation

Typically, employees in your organization operate at only 50 percent of their potential, and at times, their energy levels dip below this average threshold. It falls upon leaders seated in management or leadership roles to tap into this untapped reservoir of potential and elicit a greater level of contribution from their teams than previously demonstrated. To achieve this, leaders must engage in various activities geared toward understanding what truly motivates their employees and how to harness their latent energy. This pivotal task entails identifying actions that inspire and energize employees to perform at their best. Here are six factors that leaders should prioritize to transform average performers into exceptional achievers:

First factor

Indeed, challenging and stimulating tasks represent the cornerstone of employee motivation. Employees are inherently drawn to tasks that push the boundaries of their abilities, allowing them to demonstrate their skills and capabilities. To inspire and motivate your workforce, it's crucial to assign them challenging assignments that encourage them to showcase their talents. Moreover, foster an environment that nurtures their growth and development by providing continuous encouragement and constructive feedback when necessary.

Second factor

The second motivating factor lies in fostering an environment of open idea exchange. Leaders who dictate tasks to their employees without fostering dialogue rarely reach their full potential. Conversely, those who engage in meaningful conversations with their teams, explaining the purpose behind tasks, emerge as exceptional leaders. By ensuring that employees grasp the significance of their contributions to the company's growth, leaders instil motivation and drive, leading to a remarkable increase in productivity.

Third factor

The third motivating factor revolves around delegating responsibilities. This aspect holds immense significance in leadership. Following the principle encapsulated in the Thirukkural, "Assign him a task and let him see it through," effective leadership entails assessing how tasks can be accomplished and entrusting them to the capable hands of employees. By distributing responsibilities, leaders can efficiently elicit the finest actions and yield positive outcomes from their teams.

Fourth factor

Personal growth and advancement represent the fourth motivating factor for your employees. However, there's a common misconception that this factor takes precedence over others. While it's crucial for individuals to engage in actions that foster their personal growth, it becomes invaluable when these actions also contribute to the development of others and the improvement of management practices. Actions geared solely towards personal advancement are deemed futile if they don't serve the collective growth. True success lies in achieving a balance where personal growth aligns with the progress of others and the broader community, fostering success for both individuals and society as a whole.

Fifth and Sixth factor

Money and the work environment are often considered the fifth and sixth factors that drive people's motivation. While these aspects hold significance, they are not necessarily the primary motivators, contrary to popular belief. Money is undeniably essential, leaving little room for debate. However, beyond financial compensation, the satisfaction derived from one's actions adds an extra layer of fulfilment. I have encountered several employees disengaged and apathetic towards their work, unknowingly neglecting their talents and stifling the potential of those around them. Engaging in unproductive activities such as pointless arguments and blaming management further perpetuates a negative cycle. Identifying individuals exhibiting such behavior is crucial, as they may not be entirely avoidable. Implementing minor adjustments can redirect their energy towards more creative pursuits. Leaders must recognize these individuals and address their concerns to foster a more productive work environment.

Embrace virtuous actions as your steadfast companions

A research work indicates that consistent actions gradually solidify into habits. Cultivate the habit of engaging in constructive and creative activities consistently. In contemporary society, many individuals squander their time on unproductive endeavours, fostering detrimental habits that hinder personal and organizational progress. By prioritizing constructive actions and positive thinking, individuals can cultivate beneficial habits that contribute to personal and professional growth.

Always keep yourself open to changes and progress

Embrace change as a catalyst for productivity and effective management. Whether the changes are incremental or monumental, begin by assessing their scope and potential shortcomings. Explore various transformative approaches, ranging from adopting new technologies to initiating novel strategies. It is through innovation that humanity progresses. Take, for instance, the technological advancements of the 1960s, where vacuum tube radios and gramophones prevailed until Sony introduced transistor-based alternatives. Despite being bulkier, these new devices were lauded for their compactness and energy efficiency. Similarly, the advent of the Walkman in the 90s revolutionized personal audio devices, overshadowing traditional radios and tape recorders. Today, the evolution of microelectromechanical systems (MEMS) technology has enabled the integration of diverse functionalities into smartphones. In this ever-evolving landscape of technology and ideas, embracing change becomes paramount for continuous advancement and success.

Exploring new technologies within your company often unveils the untapped creativity of many individuals. While executives may set the overarching goals for the company, it's the employees who are instrumental in implementing them. It's crucial to acknowledge that empowering your employees to unleash their creativity is essential for fostering the development of new technologies that benefit both the people and the company's growth.

Dinner gatherings to strengthen relationships

In the Aerospace Department at Anna University, we've adopted a unique routine. Once a month, we gather for dinner to foster camaraderie, address any differences among us, and foster consensus-building. What initially began as a casual endeavour has evolved into a platform for various creative activities. These initiatives not only enhance productivity but also facilitate open communication, mutual understanding, and relationship-building. Even today, this practice remains integral to our department's culture.

Similarly, in the instrumentation sector located at the Guindy premises, similar efforts are made to strengthen relationships. Various activities such as family outings and annual festivals are organized to promote unity and collaboration among colleagues. These endeavours have yielded numerous positive outcomes, enhancing productivity and fostering a spirit of teamwork.

Consider implementing similar initiatives in your organization to nurture relationships and promote harmony. Such activities have the potential to significantly enhance productivity and collective efforts.

Let your team to carry out tasks with satisfaction

Every two years, consider rotating your employees to different departments or roles of their choice. This initiative serves a dual purpose for you as a team leader. Firstly, it provides your employees with the opportunity to gain experience and develop their skills in various fields, thereby enhancing their job satisfaction. Secondly, it offers your insight into their potential as leaders, allowing you to identify and nurture talent within your organization. In essence, it's like hitting two birds with one stone.

Prioritize the opinions of your employees and ensure that their voices are heard. Recognize that valuable insights and innovative ideas can originate from anyone, regardless of their position within the organization. Reject the notion that experience equates to superiority, as it can stifle creativity and hinder progress. Individuals who prioritize their own experience and financial gains over the future of the company may not align with your organizational goals. As a leader, it's essential to recognize and address such attitudes to avoid potential challenges and ensure the success of your company.

Adopt novel technologies

Change is an ongoing process that cannot be halted or ignored. As a leader, it's essential to prepare your employees to adapt to rapidly evolving technologies. Explore ways to integrate new technologies into their workflow and support them in embracing these changes. By honing this skill, you can enhance your leadership effectiveness and foster skill development among your team members.

For instance, in 2009, the Tamil Nadu Electricity Board underwent a complete computerization process. Initially, my father, who was nearing retirement in 2011, found it challenging to grasp computer operations. However, with a week of dedicated training, he mastered the technology and even began teaching his colleagues. Even after retiring, he continues to support his former colleagues at the electricity board, contributing to the company's growth and technological advancement.

This example illustrates how individual efforts can drive organizational change and progress. By leveraging technology to enhance their capabilities and performance, individuals can propel themselves and their organizations forward on the path to success.

Fully comprehend what leadership is all about

Leadership has been introduced in a somewhat misguided manner since childhood. Students are initially labeled as "School Student Leaders," awarded to those who secure the top rank in their academic pursuits. This approach, established long ago by someone else, rotates student leaders based on their quarterly and half-yearly examination scores. However, I believe this method is flawed. Leadership is erroneously equated solely with academic achievement, neglecting its true essence. The educational community must take immediate action to rectify this misconception.

It's intriguing to note that many students who held leadership roles in school lack such qualities later in life, while a modest number exhibit exceptional leadership skills. True leadership isn't contingent upon academic prowess or superficial actions but rather on problem-solving abilities. Students aspiring for leadership roles should be prepared accordingly, with an emphasis on understanding the importance of leadership beyond academic achievements.

Leadership dynamics in colleges differ slightly from those in schools. Here, students are provided with diverse opportunities to enhance their skills. Various student groups serve as platforms for students to showcase their unique talents and hone their leadership abilities. With the freedom to choose suitable groups and leaders, colleges, such as Anna University, boast approximately 60 to 70 student groups. These committees play a pivotal role in cultivating leadership qualities among students through activities like program coordination, team management, fund allocation, cohesive planning, and fearless expression of opinions.

Effective inter-organizational leadership hinges on adeptly managing actions and implementing plans to achieve company goals with the support of employees. Drawing upon leadership experiences gained from college groups, individuals can lead teams with vitality and enthusiasm. Seeking guidance from literature or past leaders, creating a repertoire of best practices, and consistently applying them are essential steps towards honing leadership skills.

Strengthen the basis of leadership skills and managerial skills

Alexander inherited his father's army, while Napoleon the Great ruled over the entire French state. Genghis Khan, revered as the master of military tactics, started from scratch. He disregarded his birth, past events, and future consequences, focusing solely on victory. He meticulously built the foundation necessary for success, ensuring the survival of the Mongol empire long after his passing. Genghis Khan's legacy serves as a testament to the enduring fame of those who establish strong foundations.

To excel in administrative and leadership skills, emulate Emperor Genghis Khan by vigorously developing your fundamental abilities. Polish them, sharpen them—they are your most potent weapons for success. Begin by identifying the skills you wish to enhance and engage in exercises to nurture them. Nature bends to the will of those with boundless capabilities; you must embrace action to manifest a better life and move closer to success.

****

15. Initiate the Change by Personally Taking the Initial Stride

Humans are often influenced by the leadership they witness, adopting behaviours and attitudes that reflect those of their leaders, whether consciously or unconsciously. Your employees closely observe how you interact with others and emulate your actions, often without realizing it themselves. Honest leaders foster honesty among their employees, while those skilled in time management inspire their teams to excel in this area. If you seek to instigate change within your team, led by example. Even small changes initiated by you can have a profound impact on your employees' lives.

Recently, a colleague, who serves as a center director, expressed frustration over his driver's habitual tardiness, which was impeding his work. I posed several questions to him: Do you arrive at the office promptly each morning? Do you keep your driver waiting unnecessarily by repeatedly delaying your departure? Are you providing him with adequate rest? Have you established reasonable work hours for him? I advised him to make changes in his own behavior before expecting them from others. When he later shared with me that his driver's punctuality had improved, he credited the positive shift to his own changes. Remember, change begins with oneself; without personal transformation, external change remains elusive.

Recuperate from the crumble

Exceptional leaders meticulously strategize and prepare well in advance for the journey ahead. They meticulously assess their company's strengths and weaknesses, pre-empting any potential downturns. They keenly focus on the essential steps required to mitigate risks and navigate through challenging times. Through thorough analysis, they identify the root causes of any decline and swiftly implement corrective measures. Embracing innovative ideas and cutting-edge technologies, they drive productivity enhancements. Consequently, their concerted efforts propel their company from a state of decline towards a trajectory of growth and progress.

Be with clarity

Take a closer look at companies on the path to decline, and you'll notice a common theme: a lack of clarity among their employees regarding the company's goals and objectives. What defines success for our company? What are our aspirations? Where are we headed, and what does our future look like? These questions often remain unanswered. To become a more effective leader, it's crucial to master the art of communicating your vision and objectives clearly to your team. Clearly articulate your expectations and guide how to achieve them. When your employees clearly understand what is expected of them, they are more likely to deliver the desired results.

Explain things clearly

Many employees express frustration over not knowing their company's expectations. To address this issue, during the data collection process for Anna University NAAC-2023, we introduced a manual system. Alongside the software, we provided a comprehensive metric manual, designed to be easily understood by all Anna University staff. This manual outlined in clear terms the expectations regarding information and support resources. As a result, we received the desired information and support from employees. This experience taught us a valuable lesson: clarity is key to ensuring that employees meet expectations and deliver the desired outcomes promptly.

Never argue with fools

Once, a donkey and a tiger engaged in a dispute in the forest. The donkey insisted that the grass was blue, which greatly angered the tiger. The tiger vehemently argued that all grass was green. Despite the tiger's protest, the donkey persisted, claiming it had seen blue grass with its own eyes. Unable to resolve the issue themselves, they brought it before the lion, the forest's king. After hearing both sides, the lion ruled in favour of the donkey, declaring that the tiger, for spreading misinformation, would be banned from the forest for a year. Delighted, the donkey leaped and ran off. Later, the tiger approached the lion, perplexed by the verdict, as it knew the grass was indeed green. The lion explained that the punishment was not about the grass's color but rather about the tiger, who wasted time arguing with an ignorant fool. The moral? Don't waste time arguing with ignorant individuals, akin to the donkey in the forest, who may cross your path in life.

Use the 80/20 strategy

The Pareto Principle suggests that 80 percent of your desired outcomes stem from just 20 percent of your efforts. To ensure optimal results with minimal effort, focus on the critical 20 percent of your activities. You'll notice a smoother workflow and heightened satisfaction. Similarly, when addressing issues, recognize that 80 percent of your problems stem from 20 percent of the underlying causes. By pinpointing and resolving these core issues, you can alleviate the majority of challenges. If you find yourself at a loss, lacking enthusiasm or feeling frustrated, refocus on your essential goals. These goals serve as the pathway to success, empowering you to conquer leadership and maintain a sense of vitality and purpose.

Remain on the battlefield and combat

Great leaders throughout history have consistently chosen to remain on the battlefield, leading by example and driving their nations forward. From figures like Hitler to Napoleon, their commitment to being present on the frontlines exemplifies their dedication to their cause and their people. They recognized that their presence was not just symbolic but instrumental in motivating their troops and rallying their forces even in the face of adversity.

Even in the direst circumstances of battle, these leaders refused to retreat or hide, solidifying their reputation as formidable leaders. Their willingness to stand firm, even in defeat, further cemented their legacy as exceptional leaders who led from the front.

For any leader aspiring to greatness, it's crucial to be grounded and actively involved in the action. Direct engagement allows for a real-time understanding of the situation and facilitates swift decision-making and effective action. Employees, inspired by their leaders' presence and commitment, strive to emulate their dedication and drive.

A prime example of this leadership approach can be seen in historical figures like Rajaraja Chola and his son Rajendra Chola, who expanded the Chola Empire through their hands-on leadership on the battlefield. By leading from the front, they instilled confidence in their warriors and achieved remarkable victories.

Similarly, leaders like Alexander and Napoleon attributed much of their success to their direct involvement in the battlefield. Their actions inspired their troops and laid the groundwork for their empires' enduring legacies. Ultimately, standing on the field of battle symbolizes not just leadership but a commitment to the cause and the people it serves.

Make yourself approachable

As a leader, it's essential to connect with your team directly by stepping into their workspace and engaging in meaningful conversations. By showing genuine interest in their well-being, listening to their concerns, and actively addressing them, you foster an environment of trust and openness. This direct interaction not only encourages people to approach you with ease but also facilitates valuable exchanges of ideas and feedback.

Consider the example of Mao Zedong, the Chinese revolutionary leader who spearheaded the communist revolution in the 20th century. Recognizing the importance of grassroots support, Mao engaged directly with the peasants, championing their cause and empowering them as the backbone of China. By personally meeting with farmers, understanding their challenges, and soliciting their input on improvement measures, Mao rallied their support against the oppressive regime, laying the foundation for the country's liberation.

Similarly, effective leaders prioritize spending time with both customers and employees, understanding that first-hand interactions yield invaluable insights. Rather than relying solely on information and directives, they immerse themselves in the field, working alongside their teams to drive company growth.

Take the case of Akio Morita, the visionary behind Sony, who recognized the importance of understanding customer preferences first-hand. Despite language barriers, Morita personally engaged with customers, including one memorable instance of selling a VCR in California. This hands-on approach not only ensured that Sony's products resonated with American consumers but also laid the groundwork for the company's success in the US market.

In summary, leaders who actively engage with their teams and customers on a personal level not only foster trust and collaboration but also gain valuable insights that drive innovation and success.

Act as vendors

Leaders should adopt the mindset of salespeople, constantly pitching their ideas and initiatives to both customers and employees. By highlighting the benefits and outcomes of these endeavours, leaders ensure that both management and staff are aligned with the vision of progress. This approach fosters unity among employees, rallying them towards common objectives and inspiring them to tackle ambitious goals and responsibilities. As leaders embody the role of sellers, they propel the company forward, leveraging their persuasive skills to drive achievement. Just as a skilled salesperson can effectively promote their company and its offerings, leaders must likewise act as vendors, harnessing the collective talents within the organization to navigate towards success through collaboration.

Subconscious desires and goals

There's a profound link between unlocking your subconscious desires and unleashing your full potential. Actions performed reluctantly often fall short of their objectives and can breed boredom over time. Your subconscious desires play a pivotal role in shaping your actions, infusing them with meaning and purpose. Identifying and understanding your subconscious desires is crucial to unleashing your best efforts. When aligned with these underlying motivations, your actions take on greater significance, driving personal and organizational growth. Have you tapped into your subconscious desires? Embrace the necessary steps to fulfil them boldly, as the desires of the subconscious mind have the power to fuel extraordinary actions.

Navigate towards change

Becoming aware is the initial step toward embracing change. The subsequent stage involves accepting things as they are. Self-exploration is paramount for fostering internal growth and transformation. It entails listening to and acknowledging feedback from others about oneself, encompassing both strengths and weaknesses. This process serves as the cornerstone of personal development.

Here are ten questions to facilitate self-discovery and development:

1. Are you content with your current job?
2. What aspirations do you harbour?
3. Are you actively pursuing actions aligned with your aspirations?
4. Can you articulate the reasons behind your desired career path?
5. Do you possess the necessary skills and knowledge for your desired career?
6. Are you familiar with individuals currently engaged in your desired career?
7. Are you equipped to collaborate with those in your desired field?
8. Are you prepared to make the requisite sacrifices for your desired career?
9. When do you envision commencing your desired endeavours?
10. How do you envision your life upon achieving your aspirations?

Reflecting on and addressing these inquiries can illuminate your subconscious desires and aspirations.

****

16. Time Management

Effective time management is among the foremost and most formidable challenges for aspiring leaders. The adept handling of time spells the difference between triumph and defeat for any leader. Time, an invaluable resource, is beyond manipulation, cessation, or accumulation; once elapsed, it eludes reclamation. It serves as the bedrock for all endeavours, be it creation or obliteration. The allocation of time to creative pursuits significantly augments one's trajectory toward elevated leadership echelons. Mastery over time management underscores one's proficiency in orchestrating temporal resources. Are you the steward of time, or does time hold dominion over you? This dual query serves as a litmus test for both lifestyle choices and accomplishments. Regulating time is pivotal for fostering contentment and tranquillity. If your current pursuits fail to evoke joy or prompt melancholy, recognize the exigency of seizing control over time and effect requisite changes.

Debate

Have you ever observed a debate closely? It serves as an exemplary demonstration of effective time management. Both sides, the proposition and the opposition, meticulously present their arguments within the allocated time frame, making it a well-orchestrated affair. Each team endeavours to convey their ideas succinctly and persuasively to engage and motivate the audience. What's noteworthy is the meticulous timekeeping involved; speakers must adhere to their allotted time slots, with a reminder bell signalling when time limits are breached. This meticulous planning, coupled with rehearsals and pre-event preparations, ensures a captivating and well-paced debate, with the moderator overseeing time management with precision.

In our college, we have a dynamic multi-disciplinary team known as the "MIT Variety Team," comprising around 50 to 60 students. Established in 2008, this team aims to hone students' non-academic skills, emphasizing creativity, eloquence, teamwork, and, notably, time management. The team showcases its talents at various college events, garnering a dedicated following across different segments of society. During their performances, each participant is allocated a specific time slot, typically around 20 minutes, to demonstrate their skills. Competitions are also organized to provide students with opportunities to exhibit their talents individually or in groups, all within the allotted time constraints. Ranging from entertaining skits to thought-provoking presentations, the performances cater to diverse audience preferences, captivating and engaging spectators while fostering skill development, including effective time management, among students.

Hit the nail on its head

Efficient time management hinges on diving straight into the heart of the matter without unnecessary delays. Before reaching out to someone, sketch out a rough outline of the topics you wish to discuss with them. When you make the call, courteously acknowledge their busy schedule by stating, "I understand you're swamped with tasks, but I'd like to discuss these three specific points with you. Do you have a moment?" This approach underscores your respectfulness and keenness to address matters promptly. By getting straight to the point, you demonstrate professionalism and consideration for their time, garnering their respect and willingness to engage with you. If they happen to be occupied when you call, graciously apologize and offer to reconnect once they're available, ensuring you end the call courteously. By adhering to this approach, you leave a positive impression, prompting them to reach out to you once they're free. Embrace this method, and you'll reap its numerous benefits.

Take command of your time

Execute your tasks diligently during office hours. Begin your daily responsibilities promptly upon arriving at the office. Avoid engaging in idle conversations, complaining, or spending excessive time on the internet, including social media platforms like Facebook, Twitter, and Instagram. Plan your tasks for the day ahead of time, ideally the night before, allocating specific timeframes for each. Research suggests that investing time in planning can save up to ten times that amount in actual execution. Maintain control over your schedule to ensure efficient completion of tasks without succumbing to distractions. External interruptions often pose a threat to productivity. Uninvited visitors may seek to consume your time unnecessarily. Learn to manage such encounters effectively. Minimize non-essential phone conversations and activities that do not contribute to your objectives. If someone intrudes on your time uninvited, politely inform them that you are currently occupied with important tasks and suggest rescheduling the discussion for a later time. This approach serves a dual purpose: it allows you to focus fully on your work while subtly conveying to others that you prioritize productivity over idle chatter.

Follow the ABCDE method to sharpen your leadership

Utilize the ABCDE method to effectively manage your time. Begin by compiling a list of your projects and tasks, prioritizing them based on their impact. Assign each task a classification—A, B, C, D, or E—according to its significance and potential consequences. "A" tasks represent critical actions with severe repercussions if neglected, warranting immediate attention. Ensure these tasks take precedence to fulfil your responsibilities effectively. "B" tasks are important but have less severe implications than "A" tasks. "C" tasks offer some relief and can be addressed without significant impact on your work. For instance, personal activities like watching a movie after completing your daily tasks fall under this category. "D" tasks are suitable for delegation, allowing you to focus on higher-priority activities. Lastly, "E" tasks are non-essential and should be discarded to optimize productivity. Research conducted by Robert Hop International reveals that many individuals spend valuable work hours on "C" activities that provide minimal benefit to their organizations. Engaging in such activities, such as arriving late, engaging in non-work-related conversations, or taking extended breaks, can become habitual and hinder productivity over time. It's crucial to recognize that these actions do not contribute to organizational growth or individual success. By implementing the ABCDE method and prioritizing tasks accordingly, individuals can take control of their time and maximize their effectiveness.

Plan before you start the task

Anticipate your leadership obligations in advance. Enhance your leadership prowess by comprehending your company's dynamics, employee attitudes, and strategic initiatives. As you encounter new projects and responsibilities, integrate them into your task list and prioritize them using the ABCDE framework. Refrain from accepting tasks that hold little importance for you, and strive to distance yourself from such duties. Even under pressure, assert your inability to undertake non-essential responsibilities. Recognize that indulging in unimportant tasks can swiftly deplete your time and hinder your effectiveness as a leader.

Learn to say 'no' to distractions

Create and regularly update a list of tasks you cannot undertake, alongside those you can delegate or refuse. By identifying actions that consume time and cause distractions, you empower yourself to address them effectively. Embrace the power of "no" in time management, as it serves as a crucial boundary-setting tool. When approached by outsiders requesting assistance, assess whether their requests align with your priorities. If not, politely decline and defer the task to a more suitable time. Avoid engaging in activities that lack value or detract from your productivity. Maintain a clear timeframe for completing tasks and resist taking on new responsibilities until existing ones are fulfilled. Practice assertiveness and prioritize your commitments to optimize your time management skills as a leader.

Choose the time management system

Instead of navigating your schedule aimlessly, embrace a structured time management system that suits your needs. Explore various time management methods and choose one that resonates with you. Leverage technology to optimize your time management efforts. If you use a smartphone, consider downloading one of the many online free time management apps. For those who frequently work on laptops, utilize tools like the "Automatic Day Planner" to schedule tasks and actions efficiently. These digital aids are invaluable reminders, ensuring you stay on track with your plans and responsibilities.

****

17. Comprehending Leadership and its Affiliated Concepts

Failures are the foundations of success

Leaders refrain from labelling setbacks as failures; rather, they view them as invaluable learning experiences. Understanding one's strengths renders defeat inconsequential, as setbacks pale in comparison to the resilience and determination exhibited in the face of challenges. Those who embrace failure as a stepping stone to success find themselves unfazed by adversity, while others recoil in fear. Thomas Watson, the esteemed head of IBM, once advised a young officer to double down on his failures, recognizing them as the cornerstone of growth and achievement. Indeed, the path to success is paved with a succession of failures, each contributing to one's wisdom and fortitude.

My passion for vintage vacuum tube radios and televisions led me to numerous attempts at repair, often met with failure. However, with each setback, I gleaned valuable lessons, seeking insights from experts and friends alike. Through perseverance and determination, I now proficiently repair these devices, welcoming guests into my home to share in my passion. I've come to realize that success is rooted in a series of failures, each offering a wealth of experience.

During my tenure at Anna University, an unexpected setback arose when our team was denied entry to NASA's UAV competition due to visa issues. Despite the disappointment and ridicule, I remained steadfast in my commitment to promote our university. Today, after years of perseverance, I embark on my first flight, representing Anna University with pride. This opportunity, graciously provided by Elsevier, signifies a culmination of years of dedication and resilience. At the panel discussion hosted by Elsevier, I advocated for the importance of accreditation and quality standards in higher education, earning recognition from esteemed individuals like Robert, the company's vice president. Reflecting on this journey, I am reminded that success is not bestowed upon the faint-hearted but reserved for those who persevere with unwavering determination.

Find strategic solutions

Leaders address setbacks and crises with a focus on swift resolution rather than assigning blame. In times of emergency, their priority is finding solutions rather than pointing fingers. They adhere to a set of crucial steps to tackle crises, regardless of their magnitude, that include the following.

Staying calm

Maintaining a calm mind is crucial for navigating critical situations and resolving problems effectively. Leaders understand that the future of their company hinges on their decision-making. They acknowledge that crises can arise unexpectedly, thrusting them into challenging situations where tough choices must be made. Therefore, it's essential to remain composed during such moments. A clear mind is instrumental in making sound decisions and achieving success. Hence, it's imperative to always strive for tranquillity and clarity of thought.

Have complete faith in your abilities

Regardless of success or failure, maintain unwavering faith in yourself and your capabilities. Success propels you closer to the next level, while failure enriches your experience and fuels your drive to excel. Leaders consistently confront both success and failure with equanimity, recognizing their significance in fostering company growth.

Move forward

Do not allow unexpected life events to deter your efforts. Persist in moving forward to achieve success. Continuous progress not only motivates you but also inspires your team to act efficiently. Stay mindful of upcoming events, strategize accordingly, and maintain momentum.

Gather authentic information

To pave the path to success, accurate information is paramount in crafting effective strategies and plans. Therefore, in your leadership journey, prioritize gathering comprehensive information and statistics. Understand that the key to unlocking success lies within the insights derived from the information you collect.

Take responsibility for situations

Embrace accountability for both triumphs and setbacks. Refrain from dwelling on past mishaps or shifting blame onto others. Avoid evading responsibilities by offering excuses. When ISRO's SLV rocket test encountered a setback and exploded over the Bay of Bengal during its second phase, Satish Dhawan, then chairman of ISRO, exemplified remarkable leadership by assuming full accountability. Despite not being directly responsible for the project's execution, he took complete ownership of the failure. Dhawan's exemplary conduct during this crisis underscores the essence of true leadership—taking responsibility without casting blame. Instead, he rallied his team, bolstering their spirits in the face of adversity. His unwavering belief in their capabilities ultimately culminated in the successful launch of the SLV-3 rocket in 1980, carrying the "Rohini" satellite weighing approximately 40 kg.

Firefight the problems

Recognize that in times of crisis, you are the only one capable of effectively managing the situation. Crises serve as catalysts for revealing the latent leadership qualities within you and allowing them to shine. Embrace crises as opportunities to harness your inner strength and accomplish remarkable feats.

Instead of fearing crises, confront them head-on. Prepare yourself by devising contingency plans tailored to emergencies. Thoroughly analyse and explore potential avenues for success in your projects. Cultivate unwavering confidence in your abilities to overcome challenges and emerge victorious.

Engage in constant exchange of ideas

In my view, the primary key to understanding is the exchange of ideas. Continuously communicate with both your team and management, beginning with understanding management's expectations from employees. Utilize feedback channels to convey to management the expectations and perspectives of the employees. It is through this exchange of ideas that you can elevate your actions to a higher level. Constantly engage in exchanging ideas to effectively implement your thoughts, strategies, and assumptions.

Identify your shortcomings

Identify the obstacles preventing you from resolving your crisis and take steps to address them. Only by fully acknowledging your weaknesses can you begin to correct them. How can you identify your shortcomings? Seek input from others. While it may be challenging to fully accept your weaknesses, acknowledging them and actively working to improve them enhances your leadership. Remember, addressing shortcomings is integral to becoming a great leader.

Transform creativity and imagination into action

Crafted originally for sustenance and reproduction, humans have flourished due to their boundless imagination and creativity. Initially, humans harnessed fire for protection against wildlife, later adapting it for cooking. The evolution of agriculture stemmed from this knowledge, allowing for sustained food production. The invention of the wheel further revolutionized transportation and trade. Fire and the wheel stand as enduring symbols of human ingenuity, marking significant transitions from the Stone Age to the Metal Age. Therefore, it's paramount to nurture and foster creativity and imagination, allowing them to soar unhindered.

Counterattack

The Mongol Empire was renowned for its tactical prowess, particularly its strategic counter-offensives. One notable manoeuvre involved a detachment of soldiers appearing on horseback to engage the enemy, feigning fear and retreat. As the enemy pursued, believing victory was imminent, hidden Mongol forces launched a surprise attack, swiftly destabilizing their adversaries. This astute tactic dismantled the enemy's formidable defences in a matter of moments.

Similar to the Mongol soldiers, it's crucial to assess your circumstances, channel your energies, devise strategies, and counter adversity head-on. Rather than succumbing to fear, confront challenges with determination. Identify the root causes of your problems and execute targeted countermeasures. Often, the majority of significant issues stem from a select few underlying factors, known as the 80/20 rule. By addressing these core issues, you can effectively neutralize the broader challenges you face.

Keep things simple

As leaders, navigating crises can often lead to distractions. To mitigate this, prioritize simplicity in your actions. Ensure each task is isolated, with minimal dependencies between them. Simplifying your approach not only streamlines execution but also minimizes potential complications. Focus on fostering clarity and understanding in your actions to maintain simplicity amidst complexity.

Comprehend the method of social conditioning

In leadership roles, it's crucial to deeply comprehend the dynamics of social justice surrounding you, as they can significantly impact your leadership journey, directly or indirectly. Respect for your employees' diverse backgrounds, including language, race, gender, and religion, is paramount. Consider their lifestyles and circumstances, striving to support their overall well-being and advancement.

Social transformation often spans multiple generations. Upholding fundamental rights in areas like education, the economy, and employment is vital for societal progress. Take, for instance, the reservation system—a mechanism aimed at promoting social equality. Misconceptions sometimes arise, suggesting that reservation benefits only individuals and their families. However, this notion is flawed.

Reflect on my father's journey—an ordinary accountant at the electricity board. Through his commitment to education, he paved the way for my advancement. His actions not only uplifted our family but also inspired others in our community. This illustrates how reservation policies, when implemented effectively, can uplift individuals and their surrounding communities.

Imagine if my father hadn't pursued education or if he had been denied social justice opportunities. This underscores the transformative impact of equitable policies. Reservation initiatives don't merely benefit individuals; they catalyse broader societal progress. As individuals thrive, families, communities, and eventually, the nation flourish. Embracing equality fosters societal cohesion and prosperity, reflecting positively on the nation's character and development.

Never give up your uprightness under any circumstances

Exceptional leaders consistently demonstrate integrity. They recognize that their conduct mirrors that of their employees. They understand that every aspect of their daily actions is closely scrutinized and can influence the company's reputation. Therefore, they opt for resolutions that preserve their credibility during crises and the endeavours they undertake.

Keep trying until you win

Persist until setbacks surrender to your determination. Firstly, comprehend the causes behind setbacks, then embark on endeavours to eliminate them. Only through clear analysis can you pave the way for triumph. Leaders persevere until they achieve success in their endeavours, meticulously planning for success and preparing contingency measures for unforeseen circumstances. In times of absence, they delegate pre-planned measures to the appropriate individuals. During World War II, Stalin implemented an alternative strategy known as "People's Power" to repel German forces from Russia. This historic initiative saw civilians joining the Russian army on the frontline, rallying behind their nation in the face of imminent German invasion. Fuelled by Russian patriotism, citizens took up arms and fought alongside the military, compelling the German forces to retreat within a mere two weeks. Among Stalin's notable alternative initiatives, "People's Power" holds a prominent position in history.

Think forward

The fundamental requisites of leadership entail foresight and meticulous planning for its realization. A remarkable leader dedicates profound thought to the advancement of their organization and the well-being of its members. They recognize that the company's progress hinges upon the enhancement of its workforce's capabilities. Thus, they endeavour to equip both the company and its employees for the future.

As a leader, it is imperative to anticipate future trends and engage in proactive project initiatives. Harnessing the wisdom and insights of esteemed predecessors in your field can aid in this endeavour. Regularly evaluate your alignment with the requisite planning standards and the efficacy of your strategies in attaining the desired objectives. In "Main Kampf," the book discusses how Hitler, the infamous dictator of Germany during World War II, meticulously devised his aggressive actions while incarcerated.

Sketch your plan in writing

Initiate your planning process by documenting it in writing. Complete clarity, a well-rounded perspective, and a structured series of actions are achieved when you think through writing. Here, "writing" doesn't necessarily mean using letters; it can encompass diagrams, symbols, color-coding, or any other method that suits your thought process. By thinking through writing, you can swiftly identify key priorities, areas that require significant focus, and those that warrant less attention. This approach not only enhances your productivity but also contributes to refining your planning and execution.

Think differently

Once, during a lecture, my management professor, Dr. Murugappan, gestured toward a pen and inquired about its uses. The class responded with the obvious: writing. When he turned to me, I offered a broader perspective: "A pen can serve multiple purposes beyond writing. It can be handy for jotting notes while reading, relieving an itch, improvising as makeshift ears or a whistle, doubling as a prop in games like 'rocket,' functioning as a makeshift door-locking mechanism, or even as a makeshift weapon, among other things." This example underscores the principle that any tool can be utilized in ways beyond its intended function, depending on one's creativity and resourcefulness.

In another instance, a renowned soap manufacturing company faced a challenge with its soap packaging machine. The machine malfunctioned, leading to incomplete soap packs jeopardizing production and customer satisfaction. With the demand for soap too high to halt production, a crisis meeting was convened. Among the proposed solutions, a young officer suggested installing an electric fan to blow away incomplete soap cards before they were filled. This ingenious idea provided a temporary fix, highlighting the importance of thinking outside the box when confronting challenges. Such alternative thinking not only resolves immediate issues but also distinguishes effective leaders.

Divert attention towards you

You're facing the challenge of teaching a complex subject for the first time. How will you approach it? This question was posed to me during a teacher's interview. Allow me to share a story: In a quaint town, a father gifted his son a beautiful calf when he was just a child. As time passed, the calf grew into a bull, and the son into a young man. When the town announced a 'Jallikattu' (Embracing Bull) competition, the young man participated. Having raised the calf, he knew its strengths and weaknesses, enabling him to emerge victorious in the competition.

I share this tale to illustrate that the new course you're about to undertake may seem daunting at first glance. However, like the Jallikattu bull, no course is insurmountable. What's essential is diligence and consistent effort. Through continuous practice and learning, you'll gain expertise and insight, making your semester exams more manageable. Today's students seek experiential knowledge that transcends textbooks and the internet. Your ability to mould and share your own experiences will determine your success. By expanding your horizons beyond traditional sources, you'll cultivate your unique perspective, attracting students and enriching your teaching approach. This method has guided me throughout my teaching career, allowing me to effectively navigate challenging courses.

****

18. Contribute to Task Enhancement

Your employees are driven to enhance their performance and contribute to the company's growth and their own professional development. Foster a creative environment where they can identify opportunities and feel motivated to excel. Cultivate such an environment by offering direct or indirect support to your employees' development efforts.

At the outset, let your employees know what you expect from them

Effective leaders articulate their expectations to employees from the start and stand firm in their convictions without wavering. Once employees grasp the leader's expectations, they are motivated to strive towards the company's objectives. They diligently work towards transforming project drafts into actionable goals within the organization.

Set the standards

Establish clear standards for the work performed by your employees and provide them with specific targets to meet. Assess their performance based on these standards and offer constructive feedback to encourage improvement. By engaging in these activities, you not only monitor your employees' actions consistently but also support them in enhancing their performance.

Assumptions may go wrong

Do your employees accurately comprehend the instructions you give them? Double-check to ensure they do. While some employees grasp your ideas swiftly, others do so moderately or minimally. Occasionally, due to workload, your employees might forget your instructions and key points.

To address this, encourage your employees to take written notes of your comments during discussions. By implementing this practice, you can ensure that your expectations are promptly understood and acted upon by your employees within a designated timeframe.

Provide feedback more often

Effective feedback is crucial for motivating your employees and guiding their actions. Provide specific feedback on what they are doing well and where they need improvement. Address any areas where they may be going wrong and suggest ways they can make positive changes. A common complaint among employees in large corporations is that they feel disconnected from their supervisors and lack clarity on their performance. Without clear feedback, employees may struggle to improve and may engage in counterproductive activities. Recognizing and acknowledging their accomplishments can boost morale and motivation. Encourage a culture of appreciation and regularly provide constructive feedback to help your employees refine their skills and performance. Human beings naturally crave praise and recognition, so fostering an environment of appreciation will foster positivity and productivity among your team members.

Deal with the problems calmly

At times, it may feel tempting to react with anger, lose your cool, or reprimand someone when confronted with a problem. However, the true nature of the issue only becomes apparent when you delve into its underlying causes and circumstances. It's important to recognize that the employee responsible for the problem likely didn't intend for it to occur. Even if their actions were well-intentioned, there may have been unforeseen factors contributing to the problem. In such instances, it's crucial to approach the situation in a manner that avoids publicly shaming or humiliating your employees.

As a leader, refrain from criticizing your employees in front of others. Instead, invite them to discuss the matter privately in your office. Take the opportunity to understand their perspective and inquire about what led to the issue. Clearly outline the challenges and implications posed by the problem and express your concerns. Listen attentively to their explanations, even if they offer reasons in defence of their actions. Sometimes, their insights may offer a fresh perspective on the problem.

If it becomes apparent that the employee is at fault, focus on constructive solutions for preventing similar issues in the future. Discuss strategies for improvement and set clear expectations for their performance moving forward. Merely issuing threats or admonishments without providing guidance on problem-solving diminishes your authority and undermines morale. Such an approach risks disengaging employees and dampening their enthusiasm for their work. Regularly check in with the employee to ensure they are following the agreed-upon course of action and offer support and feedback as needed.

Avoid objections

In the realm of leadership, clarity is paramount, particularly in the midst of chaos. As a remarkable leader, your ability to articulate your thoughts clearly and comprehensibly is crucial. Research suggests that nearly 80 percent of task completion hinges on effectively communicating ideas to your team. Therefore, dedicate ample time to meticulous planning to ensure your concepts are sharp and well-defined. Invest a minimum of 2 to 3 hours in planning for every half-hour of productive idea exchange. Jot down your thoughts in writing; this aids memory retention. Additionally, practice delivering your message in front of a mirror to bolster self-assurance. Employ precise language and articulate ideas, as they serve as reflections of your subconscious mind and character. These actions underscore your dedication and steadfast commitment to your vision, paving the way for clarity and efficacy in communication.

Effective leadership also hinges on cultivating positive habits. Remember, it's our habits that shape our futures, not our wishes or aspirations. To effect change in your life, you must first cultivate positive habits. The journey begins today—there's no time like the present to initiate change. Failure to take action only leads to stagnation. Every action you undertake, from dawn till dusk, contributes to the formation of your habits. Embrace change gradually, for even the most challenging tasks are comprised of a series of small, manageable steps. Consider how closely you monitor your progress after each semester exam. Your perception of difficulty is shaped by your dedication and preparation. Consistent practice and thorough understanding of the curriculum eliminate the notion of difficulty from your lexicon.

Success, therefore, lies in perseverance and relentless effort. Observe the unwavering determination of former Indian cricket captain, Mahendra Singh Dhoni. He approaches every challenge with unwavering resolve, refusing to succumb to doubt or despair. Dhoni's tenacity and commitment to success are ingrained habits, resulting in a string of victories for his team.

"If you consistently cultivate habits of success, success itself becomes ingrained in your routine."

Allow individuals to relish the liberty of voicing their opinions

Promote an environment of free expression among your employees to facilitate optimal decision-making. This approach allows your team members to articulate ideas and subconscious inclinations, fostering the sharing of thoughts and insights. However, such freedom of expression may also give rise to conflicting opinions on various occasions.

Conflicting viewpoints can manifest in two invaluable ways. Firstly, they may unveil answers to questions that were previously concealed during our exploration. Secondly, healthy conflicts of opinion often breed novel modes of thinking, propelling the generation of innovative ideas and steering the company toward growth. Embracing best practices amidst such conflicts is essential for guiding the company's trajectory.

As you venture into uncharted territories with new ideas, expect criticism and opposition from your employees. These minor disruptions are inherent to the process of effecting change. In these moments, adopt a calm and receptive demeanour akin to that of a tranquil Buddha, fully absorbing and considering their perspectives. Demonstrating such attentiveness to others' opinions is key to establishing oneself as an influential leader.

From my perspective, conflicts of opinion are indispensable for both organizational advancement and individual growth. They should be managed within leadership through collaborative efforts or administrative measures, enhancing your ability to steer the company and its operations effectively.

Keep trying

The essence of success lies in the lessons learned from failures. Each setback provides invaluable experience that serves as the cornerstone of future accomplishments. I personally endured 76 rejections in my pursuit of research opportunities at a prestigious institute in California. Despite this, I gleaned insights from each setback, refining my approach with each subsequent attempt. Similarly, although I did not secure a position after a rigorous seven-hour interview for an Assistant Professorship at the Indian Institute of Technology Bombay (IITB), the experience propelled me forward in my career journey.

In 2012, our team "Dhaksha" participated in NASA's Defence Advanced Research Projects Agency (DARPA) UAV Forge Challenge competition, comprising three rounds. Despite encountering challenges, such as being dropped from the final stage due to perceived hindrance, we persevered. In the final round, held in a dense forest area in Georgia, conventional methods of navigation were ineffective. Anticipating this, I proposed an innovative solution leveraging smartphone technology. By incorporating Skype into our reconnaissance aircraft, we successfully navigated the dense forest, earning accolades from event organizers and highlighting the importance of alternative thinking in problem-solving.

In moments of adversity, persist in contributing to the team's success, for opportunities will inevitably present themselves. This experience underscored the value of approaching challenges from unconventional angles, garnering recognition from the intellectual community and reinforcing the adage that innovation knows no bounds.

Acquire the skill

Upon completing my PhD in engineering in 2019, I encountered challenges in recruiting research students. Over the past three years, factors such as the COVID-19 pandemic and a general decline in students' interest in research have contributed to low enrolment rates. Aware that I required research students for my departmental advancement, I approached my mentor, Dr. K. Senthilkumar, seeking guidance.

Dr. Senthilkumar attentively listened to my concerns and posed a critical question: "How many sponsored research projects are you currently overseeing?" Regrettably, I had none to report. Dr. Senthilkumar astutely pointed out that prospective research students are disinclined to join without the allure of sponsored projects. Recognizing the financial burden borne by full-time research scholars—ranging from Rs 20,000 to Rs 30,000—I realized the importance of offering such support to attract and retain talented students.

Inspired by Dr. Senthilkumar's wisdom, I embarked on a proactive approach, submitting sponsored research proposals to various institutions. Recently, my efforts bore fruit as I secured two research grants from the central government. Dr. Senthilkumar's mentorship taught me not only to acquire the skills but also to impart the skill to others—an invaluable lesson that reshaped my perspective and propelled me towards success.

****

19. Choose Your Advancements

Not everyone born human is naturally driven by initiative or action; rather, motivation is often tailored to individual desires and lifestyles. To ensure balanced personal growth, it's essential to first understand your inherent personality traits and then leverage them to your advantage. Here are four personality archetypes to help you identify your type and harness your personality for leadership development.

Individuals in the first category tend to be nonchalant and unbothered by most things. While they possess traits that are generally appealing, they often struggle with taking decisive action. If you find yourself in this category, motivate yourself by understanding your actions' significance and potential outcomes beforehand.

Contrary to the first category, those in the second category are decisive and assertive leaders who thrive on control. However, they may shy away from situations where they lack control. If you resonate with this type, tap into your inner drive by focusing wholeheartedly on the tasks you undertake.

The third category encompasses individuals who prioritize enjoyment and spontaneity. They infuse joy into their surroundings and approach tasks with enthusiasm, resulting in heightened productivity. However, they may struggle with maintaining focus and consistency. If this sounds like you, gamify your actions to fuel your growth journey and achieve success gradually.

Finally, individuals in the fourth category exhibit a perfectionist streak, striving for flawlessness in everything they do. While they excel in thoroughness, they may be plagued by a fear of failure. If you identify with this type, motivate yourself by prioritizing accuracy and precision in your work.

Every personality type harbours unique strengths. By identifying and leveraging these strengths, you can propel yourself towards leadership excellence through self-motivation and personal growth.

"While motivation sparks proactive behavior, it's the discipline you maintain that sustains continuous growth"

Kick-off with simple things

Do you know the common mistakes people make when they step into the gym for the first time? It's often diving straight into using all the equipment without proper guidance or training, fuelled by the misconception that they'll see instant results. This approach leads to muscle soreness, spasms, and discomfort the next day. Similarly, many individuals attempting personal growth make this same error initially, losing interest and becoming discouraged when they fail to see immediate progress. Overloading yourself with too many activities in a short span can lead to boredom and hinder your goal achievement. Instead, break down your objectives into manageable steps, just as high jumpers start with lower heights before aiming for greater heights. Cultivate consistency, perseverance, and hard work to gradually improve your abilities. Pressuring employees and attempting to force progress is counterproductive and akin to self-sabotage for a leader. To boost productivity, focus on setting realistic yet valuable goals, starting with small victories before progressing to larger ones. Many people aim for significant success immediately, only to lose motivation when they encounter setbacks. Patience and perseverance are key to achieving remarkable success in any endeavour, requiring dedication and time.

Select your advancements through actions

Some believe that short-term actions don't contribute to achieving long-term goals, while others argue that long-term actions lack immediate effectiveness. In my perspective, the quality of short-term actions significantly impacts long-term goals. To excel as a great leader in the future, commence your efforts today. Consistent daily actions shape your growth trajectory. Merely planning without taking action may hinder your progress and impede your development.

The remote control systems utilized for Drone operations are primarily imported from countries like China or occasionally from Western nations such as the United States. My team and I embarked on a mission to develop a wholly indigenous remote control system in India. Through our diligent efforts, we successfully engineered a remote control system spanning from four to twelve bandwidths tailored to meet the diverse needs of our customers. This achievement showcased our commitment to leveraging domestic technology. Witnessing our innovative initiative, a private firm named "ZuPa Aerospace" expressed interest in commercializing our product. Unfortunately, due to logistical challenges and my disengagement, this endeavor did not materialize. Had I capitalized on this opportunity, my company and I would have been better positioned in the field of Drone Technology today. It's not merely drafting plans and models that enhance your skills; rather, it's the actionable steps you take that truly add value to your projects.

The Chandrayaan-II spacecraft marked a significant moment in my life, revealing inherent qualities I never knew I possessed. It was an esteemed occasion that acquainted me with unforeseen opportunities. It all began when "Thanthi TV" extended an invitation for me to be a special guest, following my regular viewership of their news broadcasts at home. Originally, my professor, Dr. Senthil Kumar, was slated to attend the event, but I found myself in his place as a substitute guest. This was my inaugural appearance on live television, an experience fraught with anticipation and uncertainty regarding the impending questions. Karuppusamy, the news director at Thanthi TV, introduced me to the host, a 25-year-old man of moderate stature and fair complexion. Despite internal tension, I managed to articulate my response to the initial question. Director Karuppusamy provided encouraging feedback, spurring me to follow the same spirit. As the program unfolded, I learned that the host, Parthiban Chinnasamy, was also a newcomer to live broadcasting. Our interaction during breaks fostered a friendship, and our dynamic discussion quickly gained traction on YouTube, captivating over 10 lakh viewers. Subsequently, Parthiban and I continued collaborating on hosting engagements centered around ISRO and space exploration on Thanthi TV.

Parthiban is a versatile individual, excelling as both a newsreader and anchor. His dedication to any task or goal he undertakes is truly inspiring. Whether delivering routine news updates or articulating the names of prominent figures, his unwavering focus is remarkable. Despite his busy schedule, he often discusses with me over the phone, seeking clarification on topics related to science and technology. During live interviews, Parthiban ensures that his questions are easily understood by the general audience, even if he already knows the answers himself. His recent coverage of the Chandrayaan-3 mission by ISRO to the moon showcased his exceptional skills. Individuals like Parthiban, who invest 200 percent effort into their endeavours, are exemplary leaders, guiding others through their actions. Anchor Parthiban epitomizes the importance of diligence and hard work. Observing his dedication on television will undoubtedly leave you equally impressed as it has for me.

****

Epilogue

This book extensively explores the diverse concepts and practices essential for effective leadership. In my view, leadership is not merely acquired through reading books or words alone; rather, it is cultivated through every action we undertake. Leadership qualities are honed through a variety of experiences, ranging from individual endeavours to collaborative efforts and advancements in technology. These qualities emerge when individuals exhibit balanced planning and engage in collective action. Leadership is not imposed but chosen by those who follow, often in silent anticipation. To develop such leadership qualities, one must first harbour a subconscious desire for leadership and cultivate a mindset of positivity. It requires making adjustments in one's actions and attitudes, and continuously exploring the principles and practices of leadership. By consistently nurturing this mindset, one can cultivate the leadership qualities they aspire to embody.

Frequently, new leaders may express frustration, claiming that they lack support from others. However, this perception is often unfounded. Rather than dwelling on the notion that others are not aiding you, consider how you can contribute to enhancing their experiences. Take proactive measures to put this mindset into action. By approaching this situation with a positive attitude, you can effectively garner the support of your team members. It's crucial to recognize that collaborative efforts, supported by your colleagues, are what distinguish an ordinary employee from a remarkable leader who achieves great success.

Evaluate your leadership practices to cultivate and enhance your leadership attributes. Through this introspection, your leadership capabilities gain value and ascend to greater heights. Your actions and behaviours shape your leadership trajectory and ultimately, your destiny. By consistently participating in dynamic initiatives, you attract your employees and inspire them to pursue your shared objectives. They actively contribute to the company's advancement by engaging in value-added endeavours, deriving satisfaction from witnessing the organization's growth spurred by their efforts.

Do you aspire to enact meaningful transformations within your organization? If so, it's imperative to ensure that these changes are aligned with your overarching goals and objectives. Reflect on your current position and circumstances: where are you currently situated, and why do you seek change? This process begins with introspection and self-awareness.

Embrace change as an opportunity for growth, particularly if your current environment lacks sufficient challenges or opportunities for personal and professional development. Remember, change isn't merely about altering external circumstances; it also involves self-transformation. By committing to evolve within your role and environment, you catalyse comprehensive growth. Strive to strike a balance between self-improvement and environmental adaptation. When you proactively address both aspects, your growth becomes exponential, and your endeavours yield greater success.

Challenges are what invigorate existence

Why does God subject us to a series of failures and trials while others seem to enjoy unbridled happiness? Some may question why a benevolent deity wouldn't simply grant everyone a life of bliss. However, consider the insights gleaned from an experiment conducted by noted ethologist John B. Calhoun, known as the "Behavioural Sink" study. In this research, conducted in what was thought to be a utopian environment for mice, Calhoun placed six pairs of mice in a controlled setting with ample resources, including food and shelter, to observe their behavior.

Initially, the mice revelled in their newfound abundance, breeding prolifically and exploring their surroundings with enthusiasm. However, as their numbers swelled and living space became scarce, the dynamics shifted dramatically. Faced with overcrowding, the mice abandoned their usual reproductive behaviours, turned aggressive towards each other, engaged in cannibalism, and ultimately decimated their own population. What started as a paradise ended in chaos and self-destruction, with the once-thriving community reduced to a mere fraction of its former size.

This phenomenon observed in mice can be extrapolated to human behavior as well. When resources are abundant and easily accessible to all, humans tend to proliferate, leading to overpopulation and eventual resource depletion. Nature, recognizing the dangers of unchecked growth, instils in us the inherent qualities of struggle and resilience to navigate through life's challenges.

It's believed that even ancient species like the dinosaurs, despite their dominance and abundance, fell victim to their own success. With no natural predators and an environment conducive to their prosperity, their population exploded until it reached unsustainable levels, ultimately resulting in their extinction.

In essence, the trials and tribulations we face are not arbitrary punishments but rather evolutionary mechanisms designed to ensure the survival and balance of life on Earth. Through struggle, we learn, adapt, and ultimately thrive, proving that adversity is often the catalyst for growth and resilience.

Indeed, life itself is a series of struggles, each one shaping us and propelling us forward on the path of evolution. Victory, too, is born from these struggles, each triumph a testament to our resilience and determination. It is through overcoming challenges that we ascend to greater heights, reaching new levels of growth and development.

In the realm of leadership, this truth holds even more significance. To excel in leadership is to embrace the challenges that come your way, to confront them head-on with unwavering resolve. It is through facing adversity that true leaders emerge, their mettle tested and proven in the crucible of struggle.

Therefore, let me extend my heartfelt congratulations on your leadership success. Your ability to navigate through difficulties and emerge victorious is a testament to your strength and vision. May your journey continue to be marked by triumphs, and may you inspire others to embrace the struggles that pave the path to greatness.

****

About the Authors

Author Kaviyarasu Ayyakannu hails from the quaint village of Poorumpur, nestled in the Mayiladuthurai District. His academic journey began at AVC College of Engineering in Mayiladuthurai, where he earned his bachelor's degree. He furthered his education at the Madras Institute of Technology Campus of Anna University, Chennai, obtaining his master's degree. Driven by his passion for Aerospace, he pursued a doctoral degree in Aerospace Guidance & Control, solidifying his expertise in the field.

Currently serving as an Assistant Professor in the Department of Aerospace at Anna University, Dr. Kaviyarasu Ayyakannu is renowned for his contributions to the development of the "Dhaksha," an indigenous Unmanned Aerial Vehicle conceptualized at Anna University. His dedication to academic excellence extends beyond his teaching role, as he actively participates in initiatives such as the Internal Quality Assurance Cell (IQAC), where he serves as Deputy Director.

Dr. Kaviyarasu Ayyakannu's commitment to leadership is reflected in his latest endeavour: the publication of a comprehensive book chronicling his life experiences, leadership insights, and strategies for success. Written in an accessible manner, this book serves as a valuable resource for individuals aspiring to embark on their leadership journey from scratch. Moreover, it delves into the intricacies of motivation, providing readers with a thorough understanding of its causes and effects.

Through this book, Dr. Kaviyarasu Ayyakannu elucidates the fundamental principles of leadership, emphasizing that leadership is not innate but rather cultivated through personal development. It is a guide that empowers readers to recognize and harness their innate leadership qualities.

Congratulations to everyone with unwavering perseverance, dedication, and leadership prowess who continue to pave the way for your success. May all your actions and projects serve as a beacon of inspiration for others, guiding them toward their aspirations with resilience and determination.

Dr. Agaram Rajasekar Jayanth dynamic English language educator, currently serving in one of the Anna University's Departments, in the Department of Applied Sciences and Humanities (English). With a rich background spanning over 3 years at both CEG and ACT Campuses, he now imparts his expertise at the MIT Campus. His instructional repertoire covers a diverse range of subjects including Technical English, Professional Communication, Communication and Soft Skills, Philosophy, Applications of Psychology, and Employability Skills.

His academic journey began at Madras University, where he earned his bachelor's and master's degrees in English Literature in 2007 and 2009 respectively. Delving deeper into his passion for language education, he pursued his M. Phil research in English Language Teaching at CEG, Anna University, culminating in 2010. His academic odyssey reached its zenith with the completion of his Ph.D. research at the English department, CEG Campus, Anna University, in July 2019. His doctoral work focused on the effective cultivation of speaking skills through strategic training, building upon his earlier research during the M. Phil program which centered on Group Discussion dynamics.

His prowess extends beyond academia into the realm of professional development, where he excels in preparing students for campus interviews and honing their personality traits. He has delivered numerous lectures on Communication Skills, Soft Skills, Group Discussions, Résumé Building, and Job Application Procedures. Noteworthy among his engagements was a Special Cultural Presentation at the International Women's Day Celebration organized by the Women's Cell of CVRDE DRDO of India, Chennai, as well as a Special Guest Lecture on "Integrity - A Road to Successful India" during Vigilance Awareness Week (VAW-2020) for the Higher Officials of the Vigilance Department of Air India, Southern Region, Chennai.

Specializing in "English for Research Paper Writing," he extends his expertise to post-graduate students, M. Phil, and Ph.D. scholars at Anna University, offering guidance in crafting scholarly works and meticulously proofreading scientific and engineering research articles and theses. As an educator, he seamlessly integrates innovative teaching methodologies with strategic training, fostering a nurturing classroom environment conducive to active and purposeful learning. His approach ensures that learning becomes not just a task, but a journey filled with enthusiasm and enjoyment for his students.

■■

"The world does not recognize you unless you fully understand yourself."